ACTOR TRAINING 1

SCHECHNER

BENEDETTI

JAEGER

CERF

Richard P. Brown, ed.

Institute for Research in Acting(with)

Drama Book Specialists/Publishers

CONTENTS

CONTRIBUTORS

RICHARD SCHECHNER is the founder and director of The Performance Group and is on the faculty of New York University. He is the former editor of "The Drama Review," author of Public Domain and other works. His essay is from his forthcoming book.

ROBERT L. BENEDETTI is Head of the Theatre Program at York University, Toronto. He formerly taught at Yale and is the author of The Actor at Work. His essay is from his forthcoming book.

WILLIAM JAEGER is a member of the faculty at the North Carolina School of the Arts.

KURT CERF is on the staff at the Terry Children's Psychiatric Center, New Castle, Delaware.

RICHARD P. BROWN is a member of the faculty at the University of California at Riverside. He is the Executive Director of the Institute for Research in Acting.

FOREWORD

ACTOR TRAINING 1 is not a textbook on acting. Nor is it a collection of scholarly essays on the art of the actor. It is the beginning of a free space, a safe place (such as our own workshops are when we are working well) where those most deeply involved in the difficult work of bringing process to life through craft can speak easily to each other and to those who want to know more about the training of actors. We want to speak of our concerns, our methods, our feelings: where we are and where we are going. We hope that the talk will flow freely to and from the working companies, the studios, the universities, the therapeutic centers; everywhere people are working seriously, whatever their approach.

It would be tempting to think of this series as a forum. But that suggests debate and the struggle to validate ideas through contest. Ultimately such contest closes more doors than it opens. The presentation of ideas, some of which may conflict, creates a natural dialectic where listening and understanding are primary and where, because no one is afraid to speak, everyone can find his own way to his own values, can freely espouse them and offer them, as Grotowski says of the actor's work, like bread freely given to sustain us and not as cake sold through some hype, no matter how respectable.

There is great mystery surrounding what really goes on in our acting workshops, almost a mystique. We hear of particular uses that teachers are making of Alexander, T'ai Chi Ch'uan, Yoga, the work of Slater, Horney, Berne, Laing, May, Lowen, Rogers, Reich, Levi-Strauss, of the exciting things being done with actor training methods with disturbed children, of the extension of theatre games into new areas, of gestalt, of new thoughts on the Stanislavski system. But little of this work and the ideas, experiences, goals and philosophy which lie behind it is open to us for sharing. Mostly, there is silence.

No doubt some of the silence comes from the guarding of methods, the creations of private preserves to be defended from poaching. But probably not much. Acting teachers, regardless of how or where they work, are eager when they meet to talk about what they are doing, to share in small enclaves the thinking and the insights of their work. Still, many are unsure and somewhat guarded when they feel the need to justify that work on any ground other than the work itself. The questions of validation are raised too early; so few get past the self-censorship of respectability and value to share the work in writing. Somehow what was easy to talk about becomes hard to publish.

We do not often write for each other as we talk to each other face to face. In the mind, the eager listener becomes the judgemental reader and the throat closes in silence, the pen dries. While some have overcome this barrier at least to a degree, and given us accounts of their work, most, unwilling or unable to become essay writers, fall silent and continue their work in private.

If the silence is to be broken, a number of assumptions need attacking. Here are a few:

A. That the respectability of an idea or approach is an index of its value.

B. That there is a fixed body of concrete knowledge about working with actors, held by an "establishment" of teachers and contained in textbooks.

C. That the value of an approach to training can be determined by its place in an historical tradition. (Too old/too new.)

D. That the style and form of communication between teachers is fixed by our journals and that anything which varies from that style and form is suspect and probably not worth publishing.

E. That actor training is separate from and unrelated to the inquiry and findings going on in other areas such as psychology, anthropology and sociology.

F. That actor training is discrete from the problems of our society: sexism, racism, alienation and repression.

The attack on the assumptions which cloud our investigation do not need to be polemic; it can be made more easily and more directly by opening them up to the most fundamental sort of questioning--by

reference to our experience. And as our experience varies, changes,
so will our answers.   But if we can go to our work free of the
pressure from the hardening of hypothesis into dogma, then we can begin to create a safe place. Questions can be faced as questions
merely, and not as admissions of failure to be hidden; we can create
models for work rather than what Whitehead called the "frozen con-
cretions" of abstractions turned to "facts."

Positivism is the enemy of any work which deals as much as ours does
with the tricky inferences from behavior back toward experience. To
mistake brute fact for truth is dangerous. As teachers, as human
beings, we are as divided from both self and others as our students
are and we must begin to talk freely about what this means in an
activity that cannot be validated by the tried methods of the natural
sciences.

We must start by telling each other of our experiences as best we can,
trusting that the freedom of the space will allow us to be heard. We
must not fear to sound strange or old fashioned, too much or too little
concerned with politics, social science, empiricism or philosophy;
too devoted to craft or to intuition; too centered on internal states
or on physical action. Let us say what we have to say in any way we
can.

Let us have a safe place to speak and to listen.

Richard P. Brown
Riverside, California

ACTOR TRAINING 1

ASPECTS OF TRAINING AT THE PERFORMANCE GROUP

by Richard Schechner

> The actor, at least in part, is creator, model,
> and creation rolled into one. He must not be
> shameless as that leads to exhibitionism. He
> must have courage, but not merely the courage
> to exhibit himself--a passive courage, we might
> say: the courage of the defenseless, the
> courage to reveal himself. [...] The actor must
> not illustrate but accomplish an "act of the
> soul" by means of his own organism.
>
> --Jerzy Grotowski

> The Mother is not an ordinary human being like
> you and me. She has a tremendous force behind
> her. She can do whatever she likes. She is
> very highly concentrated.
>
> --Vinnie of Sri Aurobindo Ashram

No written account of performer training can be--or ought to be--complete.

This monograph is itself part of a longer written work on environmental

theatre. In the deepest sense no written statement can substitute for

presence, and presence is the fundamental aspect of training. I believe in apprenticeship. Actual presence happens only in safe places, in moments of trust when the ego-boundaries separating individuals dissolve. Training is a struggle to make places safe and to encourage trust in the midst of a social system that too often breeds danger and apprehension. The exercises described here are meant to suggest a whole approach to performing, one that encompasses staging, playwriting, and environmental design as well as performer training. I consider this approach traditional--though it is far from the tradition of modern, industrialized Western theatre. Rather I draw from the traditions of communal peoples; the traditions of Asian theatre; the tradition of medieval and early Renaissance Western theatre; the tradition of Greek theatre before Aristotle. The roots of these traditions are in the belief that boundaries separating people are soluble; that groups are living entities; that theatre is a wholesome, collective, health-giving activity (resulting in what Aristotle called catharsis and what we call full responsivity). To study the work presented in this monograph one would have to go to where that work is being done, give over to its discipline, enter in, experience, become one with...

Stanislavski brought to the word "actor" a dignity it never previously had. He made of the actor a humanist and psychologist, a person who understands and expresses the feelings, motives, actions, and strategies of human behavior. Stanislavski deplored actors who were mechanical persons exploited by managers. He denounced lazy, indulgent, show-off prostituted actors who lived for applause. The great Russian actor-director insisted that the actor live his life "in art"--a state of rigorous training, self-examination, high ethical standards, and refined good taste on and offstage. To achieve this the actor learned how to be

4

"natural" in front of an audience; this was a complicated, demanding task.

Meyerhold--Stanislavski's pupil, rival, friend, and (virtual) successor--
turned the master's teachings upside down even before Stanislavski wrote
them down. Meyerhold wanted theatre-in-the-theatre--"style" and the
"grotesque."

> The grotesque aims to subordinate psychologism to a decorative
> task. That is why in every theatre which has been dominated by
> the grotesque the aspects of design in its widest sense has
> been so important (for example, the Japanese theatre). Not
> only the settings, the architecture of the stage, and the
> theatre itself are decorative, but also the mime, movements,
> gestures and poses of the actors. Through being decorative
> they become expressive. For this reason the technique of the
> grotesque contains elements of the dance; only with the help of
> the dance is it possible to subordinate conceptions to a decora-
> tive task.[1]

The dance is not "natural" in Stanislavski's sense. The dance is carefully composed not to duplicate everyday rhythms but to express feelings
and situations in paradigmatic gestures. The Great Argument of modern
theatre between the naturalists and the stylists boils down to this:
<u>Where is essential human truth to be found? On the surface, in the</u>
<u>behavior men show everyday, or in the depths, behind all social masks</u>?
Naturalists strive for a replication of those details of everyday behavior
that show the commoness of man. Stylists strive for means to pierce
through or go beyond the masks of everyday life so that the essential man
can be revealed. Stanislavski and Brecht were naturalists; Artaud and
Grotowski stylists. As in all Great Arguments most people take a little
bit of this side and a little bit of that side. But it is good to know
the Argument in its barest form.

---

[1] Meyerhold (1969), written in 1911-1912), 141.

5

Applying the principle of style to environmental theatre means applying the principle of _whole design_, of shaping all elements of the production to the tasks of finding out what the performance is. Whole design applies to the work of the performer as well as to the environment and text. Finding out what the performance is involves everyone in the process of training and rehearsal; the process of training and rehearsal is to start from scratch, from zero. No part of the performer's work is frozen or predetermined. It is assumed that hard work is necessary to help the performer develop his courage and techniques so that he can lay his mask aside and show himself as he is in the extreme situation of the action he is playing. In this way, environmental theatre performing is both naturalistic (="show himself as he is") and stylized (="in the extreme situation of the action").

This act of spiritual nakedness is all there is to performing. This act of discovery is not character work in the orthodox sense. But neither is it unlike character work. It takes place in a difficult area between character and work-on-oneself. The action of the play is arrived at through a cycular process in which the performer's responses are the basis for the work; the performer's own self is exteriorized and transformed into the scenic givens of the production. These givens comprise the mise-en-scene and are, in a sense, character. But the response of the performer to this given may at any time evoke a new given and change the mise-en-scene. The process is ruthless, ceaseless.

The Great Argument is reflected in many lesser debates, none more fiercely waged than that between advocates of spontaneity and discipline. Again Meyerhold, who is uncanny in his up-to-dateness.

Does the display of emotion really diminish the self-discipline of the actor? Real live men danced in living movements around the altar of Dionysus; their emotions seemed to burn uncontrollably inflamed to extreme ecstasy by the fire on the altar. Yet the ritual in honor of the god of wine was composed of predetermined rhythms, steps and gestures. That is one example of the actor's self-discipline unaffected by the display of emotion. In the dance the Greek was bound by a whole series of traditional rules, yet he was at liberty to introduce as much personal invention as he wished.[2]

One of the aims of this paper is to show some techniques of achieving spontaneity and discipline simultaneously.

Spontaneity and discipline, far from weakening each other, mutually reinforce themselves; what is elementary feeds what is constructed, and vice-versa, to become the real sources of a kind of acting that glows.[3]

During their visit to New York in March 1971 members of the Japanese National Theatre came to the Garage and showed The Performance Group some examples of their work. Mr. Mansaku Nomura did a selection from a Kyogen play. I loved the simplicity and discipline of his performing, the clarity of the gestures, the sudden shifts in tempo and voice. I asked him if everything was scored. "Yes," he said. "But what about your feelings inside the score? Do they change?" "Of course," Nomura answered. "Each audience affects me differently--and what I feel completely changes the texture of my performing. I work from the moment." This was identical to the answer I got from Ryczard Cieslak when I spoke to him about his work as the Fool in Apocalypsis and the Prince in The Constant Prince. Stephen Borst of The Performance Group defined character as "a set of physical and vocal actions constructed of relative movements and inflections."

2
 Meyerhold (1969), 129-130. Written in 1911-1912.
3
 Grotowski (1968), p. 121.

The circle is <u>never closed</u>. The score always allows the performer the freedom to express himself spontaneously. To provide such liberty, that is the function of a score.

"The actor is a human being who has dis/covered and un/covered himself so much that he re/veals (=unveils) something of man. He is the miracle."[4] I call actors in this sense--actors who are working towards dis/covery-- "performers." The performer does not play a role (re/cover) so much as remove resistances and blocks that prevent him from acting out, wholly following the impulses that come from within him in response to the actions of a role. In performing, the role remains itself; the performer remains himself. Also, the performer is equally adept at singing, dancing, speaking, moving; he is in contact with his own centers; he is able to relate freely to others. Clearly this is an ideal picture. In plain fact, some of the most interesting performing occurs around areas of resistance, places of special turbulence, where the performer's life-in-the-theatre is at stake.

Actor training in America is a crippled enterprise because it is an enterprise. Universities and schools as much as individuals guard what they have, market their own special approaches, jealously compete with each other. Instead of the exchange of techniques that characterizes a wholesome tradition, training is marked by secret approaches and special effects. So much of our critical machinery is geared for taking things apart, tearing them down, and so little dedicated to support. There are few places were students learn through apprenticeship and example, the best methods.

---

[4]Grotowski during an address at New York University, 13 December 1971.

The exercises presented here and the system that generates them are the barest beginnings towards finding a traditional approach to performer training. The freedom of tradition is identical to the freedom of a score. A score is tradition in miniature. I learned these exercises here and there, the most important influence being Grotowski. But Grotowski's exercises are not original with him. He has been influenced especially by Asian theatre, particularly the Kathakali of Kerala, India.[5] Also yoga has had a strong impact both on Grotowski's work and on mine. The discipline, flow, coordination, breathing, and meditation of Hatha Yoga make it a very fine training instrument.

But most important has been the work of the performers of The Performance Group. No matter where an exercise comes from, or what associations it brings, once the performers begin working with it they make it their own. All training is one-to-one, extraordinarily intimate, the process of giving birth over and over again. Many exercises are found, worked on for a while, and then given up; perhaps they will return later, or be done again in a different way. A few exercises persist, especially those for the body core and the voice work. But no exercise is sacrosanct.

I don't write this paper as a "how to" manual, a popular mechanics of environmental theatre training. The exercises are offered as a concrete way of understanding some of what The Performance Group does; and through the Group, an insight into environmental theatre as a whole. Also it is in the training that the problem of person vis-a-vis role is most

---

[5] In 1963, four years after the start of the Polish Laboratory Theatre, Grotowski's assistant, Eugenio Barba, visited the Kalamandalem to observe Kathakali training. Barba wrote a letter of thanks in the Kalamandalem visitor's book. "My visit to Kalamandalam has greatly helped me in my

sharply put. To learn the exercises one must study with a teacher, not a book. And your teacher has had to have studied with his teacher; and so on. The avant-garde is the most radical (=to the roots) version of the traditional.

There are four steps to the performer's process. One doesn't go up these the way one goes up a staircase. They happen simultaneously, each feeding the others; the four steps are life-rhythms like breathing, eating, sleeping; they sustain a performer without exhausting him. The four steps are:

1. Getting in touch with yourself.

2. Getting in touch with yourself face-to-face with others.

3. Relating to others without narrative or other highly formalized structures.

4. Relating to others within narrative or other highly formalized structures.

Performers skilled in these steps return to the beginnings about twice a year. They start with the most basic exercises (and what is most basic may vary from performer to performer) and play through them. In doing so they find new exercises for themselves and develop these on the spot. These new exercises are variations on themes--sometimes the variations are a long way from where the performer started. Doing the exercises means drawing on both their sources: disciplined patterns learned from a teacher and intimate impulses and associations evoked from deep within oneself. These impulses and associations express themselves within the discipline of the exercises, throughout the whole body and voice. The

studies and the research material I have collected will surely be of the greatest assistance to the people working at the Theatre Laboratory in Poland. Many thanks once again." What Barba brought back--and what Grotowski himself found on his trips to India--surely are one fundamental basis of the training described in Towards a Poor Theatre.

The movements and sounds thus expressed become new disciplined patterns which are used to explore still more impulses and associations. In this way the work is self-generating.

One doesn't master the first phase before going on to the second. There is no such thing as absolute mastery. The work is like the horizon at sea--you always approach its finality without ever achieving it. Each step of the work depends on the others. For example, a performer gets in touch with himself only to the degree that he can relate to others. Each person finds his own way of doing the work. This personal search changes as people change; and the work changes as the group doing it changes. The work is intimate, but it cannot be done alone. Doing it alone converts it into meditation, which has great value but not for performance.

Just as there are cycles in every individual's approach to the work so there are group cycles. The exercises are done in a space where individuals can see and hear each other. Even if a performer chooses to do the work absolutely alone the energies of the others pass through him. Sometimes the work is done with partners or by the entire group practicing together. There are various techniques for this kind of group work. Periods of contact alternate with periods of solitude. Doing the exercises in a space where other people are also working--and where that work makes movements and sounds--subtly but deeply tunes people into each other.

Each step of the work has exercises associated with it; these are:

1. Getting in touch with yourself: Psychophysical-association exercises, basic verbophysical exercises in breathing, moving, resonating.

2. Getting in touch with yourself face-to-face with others: Taking

in, giving over during partner work, name circles, exchanges, songs.

3. Relating to others without narrative or other highly formalized structures: Witness games, confrontations, rolling, carrying, jumping, flying, trust exercises.

4. Relating to others within narrative or other highly formalized structures: Improvisations, scenes, open workshops, rehearsals, open rehearsals, performances, scored roles.

The first premises of the work are that the performer is a creator, that the performer is a worker who must not be exploited by directors, managers, producers, or audiences. The performer's responsibilities are that he cannot be self-indulgent or lazy, he must give over to the discipline of the work, and respect the work of others. Sooner or later the work effects his daily living--drugs are incompatible with this work, as is hysterical, depressive, or other pathological living habits. Even tobacco and alcohol interfere with the work by debilitating the body and siphoning energies. The performer learns to work for himself, to kick out his feelings even when he is scared or ashamed. Otherwise, if he keeps bottled up, he will be resentful of his colleagues and the work. All this adds up to performing as a life's work.

Process--a term used often in environmental theatre--means "getting there" rather than "getting there," emphasis on the doing not the done. But the difference between process and product are not absolute. For the specta-tor the play may be a product. The task of environmental theatre is to make process part of each performance. For the performer most of his daily work is process. If he knows where he's going and how he's going to get there he cuts off from invention in response to known and unknown obstacles. A performer deep in process is satisfied with any point in his work provided he is in touch with that point. The ultimate of the work is identical to its immediacy: to be alive to the here and now, to express oneself here and now. What an immense risk that is! Those who love products value things and make things of all living beings. Those who love process value living and make living beings of all things. Choose.

Many actors reject process; they think training is something that prepares them for performing. "Once I get through this," they say to themselves, "then I can perform, and perform." But training gains in importance as the person matures. Not only is there new work to be learned, but there are habits to be unlearned, long-hidden blocks suddenly revealed. The body offers more resistance as a person gets older; each resistance must be faced, understood, dealt with. Public success also threatens the performer. The tendency is to freeze what the public applauds. Without success the performer feels bitter, with it he cultivates lies. Many young actors freeze themselves in a pathetic hope of ambering their talents. They learn too late that creativity's cake must always be eaten to be had.

Process = that state of being when the performer doesn't care how he looks or sounds, is not even conscious of the effect of his work. He gives over everything he is to the work at hand, surrenders to the impulse, seeks only to make contact with his partners. Process = participating concretely in the here and now. Process = revealing associations, following wherever they lead, to the very end.[6] Process is not improvisation or chaos. Both improvisation and chaos are useful sometimes. But process is a conversation

---

[6] Except for physical violence which I forbid not for aesthetic but for ethical and practical reasons, there is nothing that a priori should not be done on stage. As for physical violence I think there is an aesthetic

13

between spontaneity and discipline. Discipline without process is mechanical; process without discipline is impossible.

All performing work begins and ends in the body. When I talk of spirit or mind or feelings or psyche I mean dimensions of the body. The body is an organism of endless adaptability. A knee can think, a finger laugh, a belly cry, a brain walk, and a buttock listen. All the body's sensory, intellectual, and emotional functions can be performed by many organs. Changes in mood are reflected in changes in chemistry, blood pressure, breathing, pulse, vascular dilation, sweating, and so on; and many so-called involuntary activities can be trained and consciously controlled. This is no news to Yogis whose systems are based on the knowledge that the body is one, interconnected whole. Furthermore, the body doesn't end at the skin. The idea that people generate "auras" of various kinds is true. Also group energies are greater and different than either individual energies or the sum of individual energies.

The basic training in The Performance Group takes all this into account, though there is a long way to go before the work approaches manageability, no less perfection. For the purpose of training I decided on isolating four body systems: gut, spine, extremities, and face.[7] I arrived at this division after watching many performers for hundreds of hours. Time and

---

advantage to <u>ritual combats</u>. In this matter I am deeply influenced by ethology. I think man's performance behavior can be traced to roots in animal ceremony--especially mating dances and the displacement of agression into gestures of submission and triumph. See Konrad Lorenz's <u>On Aggression</u>.

[7] Of course the body can be "divided" in many different ways, depending upon one's purposes and needs. Practitioners of Hatha Yoga, for example, divide the body into Upper (head and neck), Middle (trunk, arms, hands, and genitals), and Lower (buttocks, rectum, legs, and feet).

again I saw people using only their hands and faces, illustrating play texts by reducing the art of acting to a kind of public speaking. I felt the most efficient way to help actors make contact with their bodies was to initially ignore the arms, hands, legs, and feet--forcing the actors to use their body cores.

The gut system is the source, the first house of performance. The guts begin in the mouth, nose, ears, eyes, and sinuses, focus into the throat then leads to the lungs and stomach; it includes all the organs of digestion; the heart; the liver, spleen, and bladder; the anal end urinary sphincters; the genitals. For all its many parts the gut is remarkably harmonic. Five rhythms interplay, for women there are seven: the swift, life-long heartbeat; the powerful in-out of breathing; the slow but deep contractions of the digestive system; the contractions and release of excretion; the climaxes of sexual orgasm; the menstrual cycle; the gestation and birth of infants. All these rhythms comprise the gut's primitive dialog with the outside world. Food is separated into nourishment and waste; breath is separated into usuable oxygen and exhaled carbon dioxide; seminal fluids and menstrual blood are discharged; occasionally a baby is started. Each gut system rhythm has its own clock from the more than once a second of the heart to the once in nine months of birthing. Even in sleep the body is not shut off, just more strictly internalized; plainly there is a relationship between the gut system and dreaming.

But for all this activity many people I've worked with are dead in their guts. The first exercises help the performer get in touch with himself --let him know he has a gut: a complicated, willful, sometimes whimsical, powerful, and responsive lifeline in and through his center.[8]

Sphincters. Stand with eyes closed, lower jaw relaxed, knees flexed just enough to maintain an erect posture. Contract the lips into a tight circle, relax. Repeat. Then contract the anal and urinary sphincters, relax. Repeat. Then all sphincters in unison; sequentially in different rhythms; in different combinations. Repeat lying on back, on stomach.

Touching sound. Lie on back, eyes closed, relaxed. Inhale until lungs are full. Hands over the bottom of the belly so one can feel the diaphragm working. Let the breath out with no attempt either to make or inhibit sound. Usually there is a slight touching of sound, an "ahhhhhhhhh."

Panting. Position as in touching sound. Breathe in and out first slowly and then more rapidly through the mouth. Don't cheat-- don't take a lungful of air and let it out in bursts. True panting is a way of breathing, it can be maintained indefinitely. After panting soundlessly pant with sound, each pant having its own sound. Pant up and down the scales. Pant a song.

Swallowing. Stand relaxed, jaws loose but mouth closed. Gather spit and then swallow it slowly, feeling it go down the throat and into the stomach. Take a mouthful of banana, chew it for a full minute, swallow it slowly. Trace the route of the banana on the outside of the chest with your hand.

Touching sound and panting are basic vocal exercises; the voice is part of the gut system. Through these exercises the performer learns to acknowledge the workings of his gut--breathing, salivating, swallowing, gurgling, burping, rumbling, farting, excreting. The first lesson is to become aware that something is always going on in the body. Then the performer learns that the guts begin in and around his face and end in and around his anus and genitals. Slowly the work makes connections between these terminals, moving from both ends into the middle. The performer senses that his breathing is a way of getting the outside into the center of his body, and that vocal production--of sounds or words or songs--is a way of letting the outside know what is going on inside the body. The first vocalizations are versions of gut-sounds: gurgles, sobs,

---

[8] Both the Greek and Hindu sense of center is of the navel, or of the area of the body between navel and genitals. Ditto for Buddhist opinion. The pre-natal infant is connected to the mother directly from the gut; this fact of biology is carried over into mythology.

heaves, gags, vomits, spits; then laughs, cries, shrieks; finally tones, scales, songs.

At the start many performers are unaware of their body cores, unable to locate their centers. These people must learn to stand still, to listen to themselves from the inside, to not resist impulses originating in the gut. I tell beginners to totally relax the face, forget about the hands, and express what they feel by varying the depth and rhythm of their breathing.

In each person's search for his center the director must be careful not to intrude. Some people have high centers, others low; some have off-center centers. The director must not impose his own sense of center on the performer. People with weak senses of their center are very open to suggestion; an eager director can badly mislead a struggling performer. At most the director approaches the performer with his hands, touching the performer, helping him feel the outer shape of the body.

Wherever an individual's deep center is there are surface spots at the base of the neck, the base of the spine, the navel, the anus, and the genitals that are terminals--places where body energy comes to and flows from. These points are contact areas on the body surface for energy centers deep in the body core. Body core exercises start with an aware-ness of these surface contact areas. Slowly the performer begins to follow the lines of energy from these contact areas to deep sources within the body core. The exercises include reacting to the environment through breathing rhythm, speaking words without intonation--expression coming entirely from variations in breathing rhythm and contractions and flexings

17

of the body core, especially the stomach muscles.

Such exercises are part of the second step of the work. Before learning them in detail the performer learns several basic psychophysical association exercises: the head, hip, and body rolls--all gut exercises.

Head roll.[9] Standing relaxed. Locate the joint at the base of the neck. This is usually prominent when the head is bent slightly forward. Begin rotating the head, in either direction, pivoting from the joint at the base of the neck. Do not push the head but let it fall in every direction in turn. The head falls forward, a slight energy moves it to one side until it falls in that direction, then a slight energy moves it back until it falls backwards, then a slight energy to the other side, then forward again, etc. The head rolls with no predetermined rhythm. The rhythm will naturally adapt itself to the associations; and the rhythm will change, perhaps frequently.

Breathing is deep and adapts itself to what's happening. Usually the eyes are closed.

Hip roll. Standing relaxed. Slowly bend over until the head is hanging between the legs. Shake out vigorously. Instructor forcefully taps the flat bone at the base of the spine. Slowly rise and stand relaxed. Then gently begin a circular motion of the pelvis originating from the flat bone at the base of the spine --not unlike the grind of a stripper's bump-and-grind. The pelvis is rotated as if there is something in front that it is moving towards and something behind it is moving towards.

Do not rotate the upper thighs and knees, or the whole trunk. Isolate the pelvis. Often people will rotate the pelvis too vigorously, shutting out many rhythms and associations.

Body roll. Standing relaxed. Slowly bend over as at the start of the hip roll. From this position rotate the body first to the side, then back, then to the other side, and then forward. the entire torso rolls on the joint at the base of the spine.

Hands and shoulders relaxed. Make sure the head goes all the way back and hangs loose. Tension causes great difficulties and can result in serious muscle strains.

---

[9] The head roll is a gut exercise because it does not deal with the surface of the face or scalp but with the insides of the face. The movement of the head, pivoting from the base of the neck, stimulates the digestive system and causes reactions throughout the rest of the guts.

This exercise often causes dizziness and nausea at first. Invariably people lose balance and fall. Sometimes there is vomiting --especially if a person has eaten less than two hours before work. Also there is severe anxiety because of the sudden and continuous shifts in body attitudes. When a person is all the way back he is open, vulnerable to attack on the face, neck, throat, chest, stomach, and genitals. This defenseless position is followed at once by the very protected position of the head tucked between the legs and the gut and genitals shielded by the back and buttocks.

If the body roll is done regularly, and correct breathing maintained, the dizziness, nausea, and loss of footing will, in most cases, pass. Breathe in while the head is falling back and breathe out when the head is falling forward. Do not try to control the depth of the breathing or the over-all rhythm of the exercise.

These difficult exercises are not gymnastics. There is no perfect way of doing them, no ideal model that the beginner emulates. The prescribed movements are an armature, a framework that can be discarded once the performer finds his own way. At first, however, the instructor must help beginners sense their blocks. The instructor insists that the basic movements are accomplished; that the body is relaxed; that the breathing is free and deep. Points of tension are the neck, shoulders, thighs, anal and genital sphincters, throat. The head roll depends on letting the head go all the way back, all the way to the side, all the way front. The body roll depends on letting the head go all the way back, on keeping the shoulders and arms relaxed, on pivoting the whole upper body on the joint at the base of the spine. Beginners like to hold on, to keep their heads looking forward; their breathing is shallow and forced; they are grim and silent. A common fantasy accompanying the dizziness, falling, and vomiting is that the body will break open and all kinds of horrid things will spill out: shit, vomit, urine, half-digested food, foul gasses, the guts themselves--all the dark secrets of the inside. These fears are physicalizations of psychic facts. In truth, the association exercises will help the performer spill his guts.

19

I keep talking about "associations" without once explaining what I mean. Associations ought not be defined before a performer has experienced them. Silence and teaching the mechanics are the best rules for the first weeks of work. If a performer insists, saying "I won't go on unless you explain!" keep quiet. Let him make up his own mind. If he stays or goes, it is his choice. From the start he learns that <u>this is his work, he does it for himself, he takes responsibility for it</u>.

An association is something private. It is presumptuous for one person to define it for another. All I can do is say what associations have been for me. When I let my head go, give over to my body, do the exercise without judging myself, without measuring against an ideal; and, if I am working in a <u>safe place</u>, a space where I do not fear intrusion, spying, or the judgment of others, then I begin to "think my own thoughts." For myself these have sometimes been like daydreams--fantasies of things I wanted or feared; or talking to myself; or hypnagogic hallucinations,[10] or even realities identical to night dreams. Sometimes my associations have been states of exaltation, raised body-consciousness; sometimes a feeling of ecstasy or separation from the body--like floating, astral projection, or levitation; sometimes a heightened awareness of part of my body as when I felt I was laughing with the small of my back while doing a back bend. Often I think of the exercise itself, of when it will be over, of what people think of me doing it, of how it may help me, and so on. I consider these kinds of thoughts to be blocks.

---

[10] According to Freud (1961, written 1900), hypnagogic hallucinations "are images, often very vivid and rapidly changing, which are apt to appear --quite habitually in some people--during the period of falling asleep; and they may also persist for a time after the eyes have been opened."

Association exercises are a way of surrendering to the body. They give experiences counter to the view that the mind and body are separate entities in relentless combat. There is no "mind over body" or "body over mind" in the association exercises. The exercises lead to "whole body thinking" in which feelings flow to and from all parts of the body with no distinction between "body" and "mind." Associations last anywhere from a few seconds to an hour or more. One can't force associations anymore than one can force night dreams. But there are ways to follow associations through to the end. During an association there are choices; an image or feeling (or whatever the association is) "presents" itself, then another, and another. Usually, at some moment, two associations will occur simultaneously, or a dull weariness will appear to drown out an association. The performer has the chance to choose which association to focus on, or whether or not to let the level of drowsiness rise so that all associations are washed out. The important thing is that the performer make his choice instantly about which association to follow. Because there is a choice one has the option of ending the associations by considering the alternatives. But if one chooses randomly and immediately the associations will usually continue, often in an unexpected direction. I used to think the performer should pick the more "difficult" association--the one he feared most--but such choosing would reflect judgment, a removal from the immediacy of the situation. An instant, random choice allows the performer to stay with the flow. As for a rising level of drowsiness there is no way to fight it and maintain a free flow. Instead if one allows the drowsiness full play, perhaps even falling asleep, new associations may occur.

An association ends when it ends. For me there is a sudden blankness at

the end, or a sharp return to the place where I'm working. Sometimes I
realize that the ending is false, that I've cut off prematurely. There's
no way to know for sure, and one shouldn't worry about it. Going to the
very end means going as far as one can at this time.[11]

At first doing the exercises will result in muscle pain, physical exhaus-
tion, loss of breath, and dizziness. One should push through these
obstacles. But sharp pains--cramps. stabs, straining tendons and liga-
ments--are signals to ease off. Otherwise damage may be done. Injuries
caused by over-exertion are symptioms of fears of getting in too close
a touch with oneself. Over-zealousness leading to injury is pseudo-
heroism. Properly done the exercises help each person strike a balance
between the disciplined demands of the work and the limits of the body.
The exercises are themselves paradigms of environmental theatre where
performing is a combination of the scored mise-en-scene and the free-
flowing feelings and personal associations of each performer.

I've described only three gut exercises out of dozens. The head, hip,
and body rolls are step one exercises. There are gut exercises for step
two. The step one exercises can become step two if they are done with
partners. For example, the body roll can be done with one person rolling

---

[11]
   The technique of random expression of inner states is the chief technique of psychoanalysis. The difference being that in analysis the body
   is kept generally still and the expression is verbalized. The technique is also like "stream of consciousness" and "automatic writing" techniques popular earlier in the century. All of these techniques are
   related to the belief that underneath surface phenomena resides a more
   primitive, more true (that is, less conditioned by social circumstances)
   human consciousness. This is a modern, Western version of old world-
   wide beliefs in the multiplicity of consciousness and the existence of
   many parallel, simultaneous realities. Arieti (1948a, 1948b) connects
   the way schizophrenics think with dreams and free association. He says

and another kneeling behind keeping a hand on the flat bone at the base of the spine. The kneeling performer harmonizes his breathing with the person rolling. The contact between the two performers will expand until it includes a constellation of body signals--breathing, touch, sweat, smell, vocalizations. Each person will have his own associations but these will occur in a context of expanded consciousness, in the space shared by the two performers.

Stephen Borst, who has been doing the exercises for several years, says of them:

> It's important for me to experience the mortality of my body. Everyday I begin the association exercises again and have to overcome gravity again. There is no final solution to these problems. I laugh and cry at the same time so much because of the incredible irony of the desire to be infinite--and fly-- and the absolute mortality of the body. It is finally a great laugh-cry to experience these simultaneously.

Other gut system exercises include "taking in," an exercise that relates swallowing-vomiting to what a person sees, and ties breathing rhythms to digestive rhythms; snout and tasting exercises; listening exercises in which performers translate what they hear inside their own bodies into movements of the gut end/or into vocalizations.

Many gut exercises are about eating--taking something into the body and

---

this way has a special logic which he calls "paleologic"--old logic. This paleologic is not causal, not Aristotelian. It works by linking predicates rather than subjects, and is entirely concrete. Paleo- logic creates private languages that must be interpreted to be compre- hended. Poetry is a form of semi-private language, an art form with just enough public language to make it accessible. The associations a performer has are not shown as such to the audience. These associa- tions underly the public languages of performance. Workshops and rehearsals are necessary so that the performer can become aware of his associations and in order to find objective correlatives linking these private associations to the public languages of performance. I am indebted to Ralph Ortiz for bringing Arieti's work to my attention.

transforming it. In July 1971 I ran an exercise with the Workshop

students at the University of Rhode Island that carried some of these

themes through to a conclusion. (Improvisations like this are part of

step four work).

> A circle with a clearly defined center. Everyone around the
> circle, no one in it.
>
> Someone goes into the center and offers himself as the Meal.
> He closes his eyes and keeps them closed until the end of his
> participation in the center. If the Meal opens his eyes and
> sees the Eater(s) he cannot participate further but must leave
> the workshop. This provision is necessary because the Meal
> must give himself over entirely to his fantasies concerning
> the Eaters and the Eaters must enjoy absolutely the liberties
> of anonymity.
>
> The Meal awaits the Eaters who come in any number. They make
> no noise except what is necessary for eating. They may eat
> anywhere and anything on the Meal's body, but without causing
> sharp pain or injury. They may nibble, suck, lick, and bite--
> but not bruise, draw blood, or in anyway treat the Meal vio-
> lently. If Eaters feel violence they should express it in the
> fierceness with which they chew, swallow, and breathe. The
> Eaters may undress the Meal and position him. The Meal remains
> passive--he belongs to the Eaters.
>
> While being eaten the Meal utters whatever sounds are there; he
> lets his breathing rhythms go free.
>
> Witnesses around the periphery of the circle keep silent, con-
> tacting the action with their eyes and breathing rhythms. They
> can move to observe, or to get away from seeing. They may enter
> the circle and become Eaters whenever they wish.
>
> Eaters may leave the Meal whenever they wish. When the Meal is
> alone, or when the Meal says "stop" (which he may do at any time),
> the director makes sure that everyone has returned to the peri-
> phery of the circle before allowing the Meal to open his eyes.
> The Meal then takes in everyone around the circle before returning
> to the periphery himself.
>
> A new Meal offers himself. The exercise continues until there are
> no more Meals and/or no more Eaters.

This exercise is an extreme example of a large set of exercises that relate

to cannibalism. Some of this work has found its way into performances--

for example, the cannabilistic banquets of Makbeth. Eating exercises that

come from listening to the sounds within the body and then vocalizing these and using the vocalizations as the basis of a dance took on for the Group in 1970 a definite and repeatable pattern: that of identifying, fattening, murdering, cannibalizing, and resurrecting a group leader, or scapegoat. Slater (1966) has detected the same pattern in Training Groups.

> What is particularly compelling about the attack (or the leader) is the variety of fantasy themes associated with it: themes of group murder, of cannibalism, of orgy.

I am especially interested in these themes because they are among the basic dramatic stories, found in innumerable variations in many cultures. Tragedy can be viewed as a cannibalistic sharing of a leader's special powers, the distribution of his mana. No wonder Aristotle found the effects of tragedy cathartic--working directly on the guts. I feel that the essential theatrical themes do not find their only, or even chief, sources in literature but in the experiences of the body, especially the experiences of the body in groups.

For each of the body systems--gut, spine, extremities, face--there are association exercises, partner work, trust exercises, confrontations, and improvisations. But the work is not dry, as such cataloging may make it seem. The majority of exercises happen only once. When the director understands the work he learns how to create exercises on the spot, letting go into his own impulses and associations, in this way strengthening his ability to contribute. The director risks failure along with the performers; he trains his skills slowly. It is not necessary to finish every exercise, or complete a round so that everyone has a chance to do an exercise. Work will begin, some performers will participate, and then the work may be put aside. I have returned to some exercises after more than a year of letting them stand incomplete. Occasionally an exercise is so appropriate that it is used over and over. The work is syste-

25

matic but not linear.

I could describe much of what happens at every workshop over a year's time. That would fill many thick volumes but wouldn't bring the reader closer to the essence of the work. The work congeals around specific performers whose problems and bursts of growth show themselves suddenly and must be dealt with immediately; it grows when the director is in a fertile, imaginative period; it grows when the group senses itself and peer relationships replace parent-child relationships. I am not giving here a chronological account of the work.

I start work on the spine system simultaneously with work on the gut. These two systems are so basic to performer development, and so closely linked to each other, that neither can be given primacy. (Work on the extremities and face is deferred.) The spine system runs from the joint at the base of the neck, used as the pivot for the head roll, to the flat bone at the base of the backbone, used as the pivot for the hip and body rolls. At these joints the spine and gut systems meet.

The spine supports the body core, and contains it as in a large basket. The spine is not rigid; it is flexible, supple, like a strong tree that gives in wind. Chronic back trouble plagues more performers than any other complaint. Backs are stiff, locked, tight; there are pulled muscles, spasms, wrenches, and vague, persistant pains at the base of the spine. Sometimes the cause of back troubles is a weak set of stomach muscles. But often back complaints are psychogenic. The base of the spine and its surrounding musculature is a magnet for every kind of anxiety and archaic fear. The spine exercises contact these fears,

helping the performer to grow aware of them and confront them, working
through them. Sometimes it's as easy as bringing an association out to
be recognized, and then the back muscles relax and the body is liberated.
Usually it's not so easy. There are three kinds of association exercises
for the spine: bends, balances, and separations.

Bends. Mechanically these are simple--the difficulty is in doing
them slowly and not blanking out on the associations. Breathing
should be free, the performer should make whatever sounds he wants.

Note: few people can do these exercises completely at the start.
Don't strain. Do as much as possible. As time passes there will
be improvement. The exercises develop self-trust if done easily
and persistently. Letting-yourself-do-it is as important as
being-able-to-do-it.

Kneeling back bend. Kneel with the thighs, buttocks, and back all
in one line. Then slowly, vertebra by vertebra starting from the
base of the neck, go over until the head touches the ground in
front of you. Keep the head relaxed, the shoulders and arms
relaxed. Breathe through a slightly open mouth.

Then slowly, vertebra by vertebra, lift with the energy coming
from the joint at the base of the spine. Continue upward past the
upright starting position, let the head fall back, and slowly bend
backwards until the head touches the ground behind you. Keep the
back arched, and the shoulders and arms relaxed. Once the head
is touching the ground slowly rotate it as far as possible to one
side and then to the other.

Then lift, maintaining the arch in the back. The energy center is
the small of the back, as if you're being gently pushed up. Use
the muscles in the back and stomach, not in the thighs and shoulders.
Do not swim up, flow up.

Repeat several times.

Standing back bend. This is the same as the kneeling back bend
except that the performer is standing. Drop the body core forward
until the head is between the legs. Then lift yourself, vertebra
by vertebra, beginning at the base of the spine, until upright.
Let the head fall back, and slowly bend backwards, keeping shoulders
and arms relaxed, until the hands touch the floor. Then support
yourself with the hands, maintaining an arch in the back, making a
full, round bridge.

Then lift, maintaining the arch in the back. The energy center is
the small of the back.

Repeat several times.

Note: These bends usually cannot be done completely at the
start. Go back as far as is comfortable, and as far as one
can recover using the muscles of the back and stomach.
Steadily, over the weeks, the performer will be able to go
back further until the entire movement is possible.

The kneeling and standing back bends make excellent partner exercises.
Give over to the partner who does most of the muscle work. In the kneeling back bend especially the partner straddles the one bending and carefully lets him down. Then, after the head has touched the ground and
been rotated, the performer's head is lifted a few inches off the ground
and the whole torso is vigorously bounced up and down. The partner is
careful not to let the other's head hit the floor. Both people let out
sounds. A variation of the standing back bend is for the partner to help
the other come from the first position to the upright position by gently
rotating the head and making certain that the neck muscles are relaxed.
Then, when the performer is upright, the partner literally drops the
performer's head back, cradling it so that there is no muscle pull.
These exercises--somewhere between step two and step three work--build
trust; they ought not to be done by people who do not trust each other.
There are other exercises to initiate trust and confront mistrust.

Balance exercises are all well-known. From Yoga there are various head-
stands, shoulder stands, and tree poses. Always the temptation is to
rush through the balance exercises, showing off how well one does them.
In fact, the balance exercises are excellent meditations. Also, when one
is upside down it is comparatively easy to sense the separations between
the vertebra, tensions in the shoulders, chest, pelvis, spine, and legs.
Each tension can be relaxed while maintaining balance. Upside down the
body is like a set of children's blocks, each standing on the other rather

precariously. The job is to build the blocks higher, in different arrangements, and then to move them around all without toppling.

Each exercise evokes different associations in each performer--but there is one associational pattern I have observed repeatedly during the headstand. When a group all stand on their heads together and begin talking to each other, they seem to become children between the ages of 5 and 8. Voices rise in pitch, giggling begins, tensions subside, and a special euphoria takes over.

Separations help performers experience different parts of the body as individual units. Particularly helpful are lifting the torso from the bottom of the rib cage and rotating it first to the left and then to the right; lifting the shoulder from a relaxed, or bottom position, to a middle position, to a high position; turning the neck sharply from center to either hard left or hard right; rotating the whole torso as far as possible to the left and to the right while keeping the arms at shoulder level and moving the head either in the direction of the rotation or in the opposite direction.

Let me emphasize that these are association exercises, not gymnastics. Nothing is worse for the performer than "movement exercises" or abstract "body work." Don't treat the body as a thing. Your body is not your "instrument," your body is you.

The third system is the extremities--shoulders, arms, elbows, wrists, hands, fingers; thighs and buttocks, legs, knees, ankles, feet, toes. There are exercises for each of these. Some can be done simultaneously with exercises for other body systems. For example, one may do the hip roll and a hand roll at the same time. In fact, the exercises for the extremities are, in part, variations of exercises for the gut and spine systems. The extremity exercises are rolls, shakes, wiggles, throws, grasps, and separations. It is important that the performer understand the amount and complexity of the creative work a hand, a foot, or a finger can do. Because people are so naturally expressive with their hands--hands and speech are intimately linked--they forget that the hands can be developed as independent, primary means of communication, as indeed they are for the deaf or in the mudra system of Indian theatre. In some cultures the feet are almost as well-developed as communicators as the hands.

Exercises for the face start with total relaxation of the facial mask. And a mask is exactly what the face is. Early in life people learn to "put on a face," and the repertory of faces grows until it is nearly endless. Each person has an extensive repertory with limitless variations adapting automatically to the situation at hand. Among the apparently well behaved American middle class, politeness often = controlling the face so that little or no expression shows. A model of American heroism is the "poker face," a blank expression concealing all feeling. Anyone who, as an adult, has re-examined the way he uses his face is bound to have discovered his own cliches, as unmistakable as his handwriting. To relax the face one lets the lower jaw go slack, mouth slightly open, with no attempt to control drooling. Breathing is deep, eyes droopy, cheeks patted loose. Many exercises retain a relaxed face as a way of encouraging body core expression. But other exercises work on the face mask itself.

Pulling in, stretching out. Two performers sit opposite each

30

other. A. begins to work his face into a dog-like snout.
He closes his eyes, tenses and points his lips, sucks his
chin in, collapses his cheeks, etc. B. helps him by telling him what parts of his face needs working. Both performers use their hands to help A. mold his face. As soon
as A. has pulled in as much as he can he slowly, step by
step, relaxes his face, letting it pass through a normal
mask and then into a stretching out--making everything as
wide as possible: gaping mouth, stretched cheeks, bugged
eyes, raised eyebrows, extended neck. Again B. helps.
Then B. does the exercise with the help of A.

The face exercises can be extended to the whole body which takes on the

qualities of the facial masks. Sound and movement are produced naturally

as a consequence of the total physicalization. Making these extreme

masks by the entire group at once can lead to extraordinary improvisa-

tions and confrontations.

A variation of the face mask exercise is the circle walk.

A large circle with people guarding whatever danger areas there
are so that the performer doing the exercise can feel completely free.

A. begins walking in a circle. Each thing the director
notices about him he says and A. exaggerates that aspect.
For example, if the director says "You're leaning to the
left," A. leans as far to the left as he can without falling.
If the director says "Your chin is jutting out," A. juts his
chin as far as he can. Once a gesture or a move is begun it
is not dropped. As A. moves in a circle he exaggerates himself more and more fully until he achieves paroxysm and collapses. Then the whole group comes to him and comforts him.

The circle walk is an exercise whose duration is brief because it is so

cruel and intense. Meyerhold would, I think, call the exercise grotesque.

Only rarely are associations or gestures uncovered by the exercises re-

tained for performances. The main purpose of the exercises is to help

people get in touch with themselves, find relationships with others,

develop group consciousness, relate inner states to outer states. The

exercises are a way of limbering up the association process so that the

performer will be able to let his feelings flow freely during performances.
The exercises help the performer feel more comfortable with sudden, sometimes unpredictable, changes in mood and expression; swift flashes of
anger and joy, and the majestically capricious manner in which body states
evoke feeling states and vice-versa. I say capricious because changes
occur suddenly, unexpectedly, making connections that are as refreshing
as they are far-fetched. Links that couldn't possibly be thought up,
images that couldn't be invented, happen and stick. In a real way the
performer is broadened and deepened, his self-awareness grows. Ultimately, the score of a performance works the way the exercises do: as
evocative circumstances within which dangerous and astonishing connections are made not by effort, cunning, or pre-planning, but in the
natural flow of events, as if by accident. The greater the separation
between cause and effect the better. In doing the work the performer
concentrates entirely on causes, on following the process through. What
it looks like, what it sounds like is of no matter to him. These things
are considered later, during discussions of the work; they are the primary province of the director who keeps a trained outside eye on the
effects of the work and the possible use of these effects in a mise-en-
scene.

Thus far I've described exercises which pertain mostly to the first step
of performer development. The second step--getting in touch with yourself
face-to-face with others--means expressing what's in one even though
there's another person facing you, watching you. That's a very hard
thing to do--it means keeping the in-touchness of the first step, with
open channels throughout the body, while being conscious of another person,
a living being outside of one's body. This other person is also main-

taining his in-touchness in front of you. The relationship between the
two people is not <u>dialog</u>. The performers are not trying to say something
to each other. Each is simply expressing himself, doing what he did
during the first step. Dialog is give-and-take, being face-to-face is
all give: training the performer to express himself without fear of
judgment, his own or another's. Trusting himself to be himself here and
now in front of another.

In the theatre, at least, a performer has to trust his partners. Once
there is trust almost anything can heppen. Before one can trust others
you have to learn to trust yourself. The first step of performer development takes the most time because it is so difficult for a person to
learn to trust his own impulses. The second step expands the circle
of trust to include at least one other person. It is important that
while working on this second step the performer not "act" or "pursue
objectives" or in any way mask his personal commitment, or ease over the
difficulty of what he is doing. A simple starting exercise of step two
work--an exercise I often use at the first workshop--is the name circle.

>Everyone sit in a circle. One person names the others, one
>at a time, taking enough time to look at each person care-
>fully, readjusting breathing rhythms and body behavior. If
>there is a mistake, a lapse, or a change in name these are
>corrected by the person whose name has been forgotten, mis-
>pronounced, distorted, or mistaken. After one person finishes
>naming everyone, another begins.

Sometimes people take new names, or are given new names, that stick. The
names of the characters in <u>Commune</u> were found in the name circle, and the
exercise itself was part of the performance for nearly a year. The name
circle is an exercise that can be done repeatedly, especially to relax
tensions and bring people back to a basic corroboration of each other.
Sometimes a person going around the circle forgets to name himself. He

33

should be told "You have forgotten someone."

A somewhat more complicated step two exercise is dressing and undressing.

> Everyone puts an article of their clothing in the center of
> a circle and then sits around the circle. A person goes to
> the center and begins telling a story about himself. As he
> talks he takes off some or all of his clothes and puts on
> as much or as little of the clothing in the circle as he wants.
> He wears the new clothing either conventionally or in new
> ways--a T-shirt as pants, for example.

> The performer concentrates on changing clothes, not on the
> story he is telling which therefore may become halting,
> rambling, incoherent.

> When there are no more clothes in the circle, or when no one
> enters to tell a story, this phase of the exercise is over.

> Then people go to those whose clothes they are wearing and
> return the clothes by slowly undressing and handing the arti-
> cles back to their owners. Everyone dresses in his own
> clothes.

Most people have trouble telling their story while sorting through the

clothes, dressing, and undressing. However, when they give themselves

to the action of the clothes their story gets freer, more self-expressive,

less set-up; it takes on the rhythm of the story-teller. The costume

assembled by the performer also reflects his mood, and frequently fishes

things from far inside.

In dressing and undressing the director reminds the performer to keep

exchanging clothes as long as he is in the center, and to keep talking.

Even if the performer is "talking nonsense" the director persists in

urging him to continue; it is frequently in nonsense that the most power-

ful associations occur. Also, while the performer's conscious attention

is occupied by a simple task, deeper things come through.

Neither the name circle nor dressing and undressing stretch language toward song or bring into play the parts of the body where breath, guts, and speaking converge. The confrontation hip roll does.

> Two people face each other, about three feet apart. Each begins the hip roll. After a few seconds each person begins to speak words. These words are not spoken to the other, they are not dialog. They are spoken in front of the other person, with the eyes open and looking at the other person. Energies flow back and forth but not as dialog.

Confrontation hip roll is the fundamental verbophysical exercise. The presence of the other stimulates a response; a feedback situation develops. The responses are in words because the process of the exercise is to give verbal life to physical impulses, to allow the performer to distort the sound of words while not losing the ability to say words.

Glassy eyes, looking away, shut eyes, stopping the roll, dialog or anger at the director, dialog with the other performer all indicate blocks. Patience and persistence is the best course for the director to take. Sometimes a bitter confrontation between one or both of the participants and the director is unavoidable. Then the director must not hold back his feelings, whatever they are. When carried through, the confrontation hip roll releases tensions from a deep level, often a sexual level, and the performer reveals things--to himself as well as to others--that he maybe was unaware of. The confrontation hip roll is the first exercise using words where the performer discovers what he feels while he is doing the exercise. It is in the realm of dis/covery rather than expression.

Another verbophysical exercise is the open sound.

> A performer goes to the center of the circle, lies on his back, eyes closed. Others go to him, touch him at places of tension, talk to him, helping him relax and getting his

breathing in touch with his feelings. Then the performer touches sound; the sound should come through unobstructed. If there is a catch in the throat, or anywhere, a tightness in the chest, a failure to breathe deeply, the others tell the performer about it.

The performer's head is tilted back so that the air passage from throat to lungs is absolutely straight. Often, as he continues to make sounds, he is lifted onto the back of one or two others and bent over so that the spine is relaxed and the body lays in an arch. Sometimes he is lifted and carried, jogged slightly. Someone is always near his neck and head supporting them so that the performer can relax completely. Others are near his stomach and genitals. There is a great deal of touching, pressing, stroking, and whispering.

The sounds that come out of the performer are often very deep and perhaps frightening if one has not heard them before. A backlog of sounds is run: tears, sobs, laughter, shrieks. Sometimes it is not possible to tell if the person is belly-laughing or belly-crying.

The exercise frequently goes through two or more complete cycles of rising and subsiding sounds. The director must be careful not to cut the exercise off short. The rhythms of the completed exercise are:

> lying back and breathing--soft sound--tilting head
> back and louder sounds--lifting--carrying--very
> loud sounds--putting down--sobbing/laughing--
> relaxed, quiet breathing

When the performer is exhausted, literally empty of sounds, and is put down for the last time he is asked to open his eyes and take in the others one at a time. Someone kneels at the performer's head so that he does not have to use any muscles other than his eyes to go around the circle. Contact is maintained until everyone has been taken in.

No rush. A single performer may take as long as a half-hour with this exercise.

Other verbophysical exercises are song and dance and foot song.

Song and dance. Everyone lie on their backs. Then one person rises and sings a verse of a well-known song. Those who know the song sing along, but only one verse. Than another person, another verse, and so on, with less and less time between verses until there is a spontaneous flow of song to song.

With each song a movement, a follow-the-leader with the originator of the song being the leader and those who sing along as the followers.

Ultimately there develops a flow of songs and dances which is spontaneous yet familiar.

Foot song. Everyone lie on their backs. One person up at a time. This person touches ones lying using only his feet. He talks-sings while touching people with his feet. Words are not thought-out. People on the ground make sounds without words. The person standing has his eyes open, others have their eyes shut.

After everyone has been the person using feet, everyone gets up together, eyes closed, sensing each other only by using bodies and feet, no hands or faces.

Each of these verbophysical exercises are part of a comprehensive verbophysical wheel. Every kind of sound on the wheel is connected to all the other sounds; and each is a function of breathing/moving, the wheel's hub.

An exercise using the wheel directly is to have each performer go around the wheel in either direction without jumping any stop. The wheel is a way of summarizing what the voice can do, and how each action is related to the others. Verbophysical training goes on at the same time as psychophysical training.

An interesting step two exercise that combines speaking and doing is locating a relatiionship in the body. This exercise is from March 1970, when the Group was first dealing with the problem of "body thinking."

> After the association exercises everyone squat. One at a
> time people go to others and say something. The director
> helps people find the places in their bodies that the words
> show in or relate to.

This exercise works out differently every time it is done. In April, 1970:

M. to W.: I have trouble dealing with my mortality.

Director to M.: What do you mean?

M.: I can't explain it. (Pause) It's about death, about time.

Director: Where do you feel it in your body?

M.: I don't know exactly. I feel high. Like I'm floating.
(He breathes deeply.)

Director: Where else?

M.: In my knees.

Director: Let it gather there, let the feeling come together
there. Deal with your mortality and death from your knees.

(M. slowly collapses from his knees and falls over hard on the
floor, ending spread-eagled, legs very stiff.)

. . . .

S. to L.: I blocked you out and I don't want to. (This spoken very
quietly, almost as if taking it back or talking to himself.)

Director: Shout. (S. does) Louder. (Director helps S. into a back
bend to open his voice.) Now, again. (S. shouts from this
position and makes contact.)

L.: (Shouting back, but his words are slurred.) I don't want to
either!

These confrontations are banal, they are not the great poetry of drama.

But feelings acknowledged no matter how banal are the sources of genuine

performing no matter how poetic. The greatest block is fear--fear of

seeming banal and trivial, fear of appearing foolish, fear of shame.

Once the performer is able to give up his mask of being special and great,

and his mask of being polite and in good taste, and his mask of I won't let myself be found out he is ready to start experiencing the feelings

of sublime poetry. Yeats:

> I must lie down where all the ladders start,
> In the foul rag-and-bone shop of the heart.

Step three of the performer's process is relating to others without

narrative or other highly formalized structures. Step three is about

trust, relating, witnessing, and sharing.

> <u>Making friends</u>. Go to someone in the room, take him to another
> place in the room that is safe for you, play a game with him
> that is fun for both of you.

Not so easy, most of the time making friends ends amid a ruin of small

talk and awkwardness or pretended fun. Lives are spent pretending we're

enjoying a situation in which we share space with people we don't know.

Step three goes back to the beginnings of relatedness.

Simple movement exercises help people tune into their partners.

> <u>At his pace</u>. A person begins to walk or move around the space.
> Someone joins and tries to move at the same pace. This is
> not slavish imitation but a try at getting inside the movement
> of the other, giving yourself over to the other.

> <u>Looking back</u>. A person crosses from one side of the space to
> another. A second person does the same. Their paths cross.
> After passing each other both stop, turn, look back, take each
> other in, and continue on their ways.

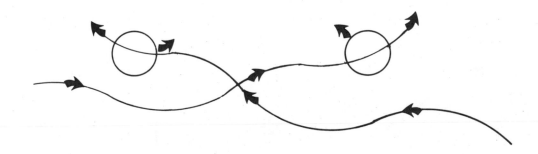

Blind leader. Someone is blindfolded and put in the center
of the group. The others protect him from danger. The
blind person leads the others. They surround and follow the
blind leader. The leader doesn't know where he's going
because he's blind. The others follow a blind leader for
whose safety they are responsible.

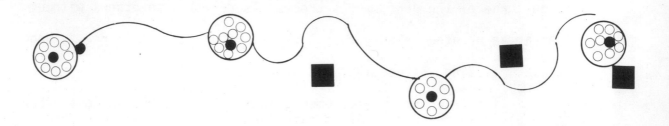

Surge. Everyone stand against a wall. One person on impulse
moves to another wall, or large object in the room. Everyone
follows, moving in the same way as the first person (walking,
running, crawling, etc.). Everyone bunches up, breathes
deeply, relaxes, spreads out. Someone else moves on impulse,
and so on.

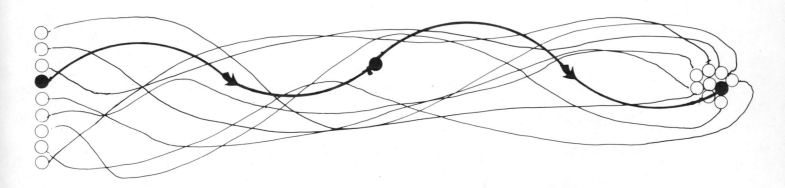

Swarm. A leaderless group moving together at the same speed in
the same manner.

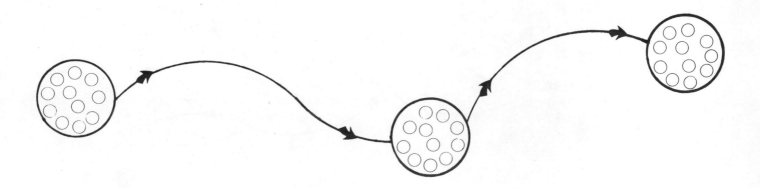

40

These simple exercises put people in touch with each other, with the group. Other exercises such as trust or flying help performers learn the physical basis of trust.

> Trust. Group forms a tight circle no more than five feet in diameter. Someone goes to the center, closes his eyes, and begins to fall in one direction or another, maintaining enough rigidity in his body so that he topples over like a tree. He is caught by the others, returned to an upright position, passed around the circle, lifted overhead, etc.

> Flying. Group lines up in two columns facing each other, arms outstretched forming a landing cradle. Someone goes to a high place, five to eight feet, and jumps off into the arms of those waiting.

The Living Theatre used flying in Mysteries and The Performance Group uses it in Commune. Many exercises can be invented from the principle that the individual needs the group and that each member of the group needs every other member. If this is not true it is good to find out early and take the necessary steps.

A more complicated situation is one in which the feelings and fantasies regarding group trust are given play. Hostility, aggression, resentment, betrayal, and anger are all possible outcomes of doubts regarding trust. Hidden affection is also the result of doubts regarding trust. Self-pity, which is usually a compound feeling, needs to be broken down into its components of affection, betrayal, and anger.

> Rolling. A rectangle of mats about 30 by 15 feet. A person presents himself by lying down on one of the ends of the rectangle. He closes his eyes and relaxes. He puts his hands over his head so as not to roll on them. Three or four others come to him and begin rolling him. They roll him up the rectangle to the other end, stop, and then roll him back. They are careful not to roll him off the mats, twist his body, pull his hair, etc. The person being rolled makes whatever sounds are there. The rollers are silent. The exercise continues until there are less than three rollers or until the one being rolled says "stop." Then another person presents himself, and so on.

I first did rolling at Goddard College in September 1970. Resentments
had been building and tempers were short. There were some direct confrontations among members of the Group but bad feelings persisted. One performer in particular felt she couldn't trust the others. I asked her to
pick three people she trusted least and three she trusted most. Then
she was the one rolled with the three people she trusted most rolling
her. As the exercise went on, I substituted the three she trusted least.
The substitutions were done in such a way so as not to disrupt the
rhythms of rolling. When she opened her eyes at the end of the exercise
and saw that she had been handled by the "unsafe" people she cried. "I
didn't know you from the others," she said. Often feelings of mistrust
are projections of one's own doubts and fears.

Part of step three is to bring others into your world, not just to do
something in front of them but to do things in relation to them or with
them.

> Witness. After finishing the association exercises everyone
> goes into a squat. No one can see more than a small circle
> around his feet as heads are kept down. No peeking.
>
> A person gets up, chooses any number of others--from no one
> to everyone--arranges them in any way, and then does something
> in front of them, or with them. The act may relate directly
> to the witnesses, like embracing, or it may simply be something
> the person wants the witnesses to see. The person doing the
> action is free to use sound. The witnesses remain silent
> unless told by the person to make sound.
>
> When the person is finished, and all witnesses have resumed
> squatting, he squats and says, "done." Someone else rises and
> begins.
>
> Note: the director must participate in this exercise. No one
> can be outside it. The only witnesses are those chosen by
> each person.

Because of the nature of witness I will not report anything I have

seen except to say that the actions are sometimes extreme and revealing.

Things come out that otherwise would remain concealed for months, if not permanently.

Witness raises three points not directly tied to any particular step of performer development, but important to them all. (1) no reprisals or blackmail; (2) no judgments; (3) non-participation of the director in the exercises. Only in regard to the first point may I be absolute. The work will not advance if people gossip about it outside of workshop, using workshop as a way of getting information to be used at other times in other places. Workshop must be treated by all as a relationship like that between lawyer-and-client or priest-and-confessor. A few words of gossip can ruin a month's work.

On the other hand whatever reactions occur during the workshop--no matter how personal these reactions are--ought to be expressed in the here and now of the workshop. It is a very delicate matter how. In outward appearance there may be very little difference between support and judgment; but in effect there is all the difference in the world. Generally, those watching an exercise do not express their reactions visibly or in sound. Most reactions can be translated into breathing rhythms. These will usually not disturb those doing an exercise. Sometimes, however, audible and visible reactions are good--these can support persons going through difficult passages. What is to be avoided are claques and other forms of self-indulgence, or sneers and other forms of put-down judgments. Occasionally, even in the midst of an exercise, someone feels he must interrupt. He should do so clearly and plainly. Then either his interruption will be accepted--made part of the exercise--or rejected. Most often it is preferable to set aside the natural rhythm of give-and

-take and put things in sequence. This way each person has a chance to have his say-and-do to the utmost. Once a person, or team, is done then another can enter the exercise, feeding feelings directly into the work. These matters are subtle, and nothing of what I've said ought to be considered absolute.

As for the participation of the director in the work, I strongly believe he should enter only when the exercise cannot be done without him, as in Witness, or when it does not need his attention, as when an experienced group is doing the initial psychophysical exercises. When there is more than one director in a group then, of course, the directors not directing may participate. However, I don't think directors should drop in on the work to find out what it's like or to learn more about the performer's process. These admirable intentions should be systematically worked out by the director in someone else's workshop where the director can genuinely be one of the performers. The director's wish to temporarily divest himself of his authority and become "just one of the performers" is arrogant and self-agrandizing. The performers work daily to develop their skills. The director serves them best by functioning as the outside eye or the intervening helper. He is not entitled to the role of king-in-disguise.

If witness is a public showing, boatrock is a secret sharing.

> Two persons sit on the floor facing each other, their legs over each other's thighs and their hands grasped at the wrists so that as one goes down on his back the other is pulled up into a sitting position. They begin rocking each other, not helping but becoming dead weight so that both persons tire quickly. When both are exhausted they fall into each other's arms. One person begins telling a story to the other. This story must be true, secret, a kind of confession: a story the teller doesn't want to tell out loud. When A. is finished the partners

44

rock again. Then B. tells his story.

Boatrock is an exercise in dialog, fundamental stage communication. It
is also an exercise in trust and giving over to another. Like all step
three exercises, boatrock is collaborative.

Sharing has its aggressive side too. Relating to others includes getting
angry at them, confronting them. There are various ways of confronting.
A person can "call a circle" and say what's troubling him so all can
hear; he can get alone with the person he wishes to confront; he can
translate his feelings into sound and movement; he can inject his feelings
directly into whatever work he is doing. The only thing a performer ought
not to do is to stuff his feelings; blocking anger takes a great deal of
energy and many other feelings are blocked in mobilizing this energy.
In all but private confrontations there is a formal organization to
guarantee that each person has his say and that the communication is two-
way. One of the riches confrontation exercises is ritual combat, developed from ideas of Konrad Lorenz.

A combat zone is marked out, usually a circle about 20 feet
in diameter. A. comes to the center and issues a challenge
by means of a dance. If the challenge is not taken up, A.
retires. If it is taken up A. and B. perform a display
dance face-to-face with each other. People on the sidelines
choose sides, show their preferences.

Combat starts when both A. and B. are finished dancing. No
rush, no surprise attacks. Combat involves sound, movement,
and total body commitment, but not physical touching. Each
time a combatant strikes the other receives the "blow" in
his body, from a distance. The wounded one then responds.
There are no misses, every blow wounds. Once a combatant is
wounded he bears the wound until the end of combat. Every
combat ends in the death of one or both combatants.

For example, A. thrusts with his left arm in a piston-like
motion. A. continues this motion for the entire fight. B.
is wounded in the stomach and doubles over. B. remains
doubled over for the entire fight. From his doubled over
position B. delivers a kick which breaks A's shoulder.

45

A.'s shoulder is slumped, his other arm continues to thrust
in the piston motion; A. delivers a kick which downs B.,
breaking one leg. From this disabled position B. bites A.
on the ankle. A. falls, and so on.

Because of the totality and intensity of commitment the
combat doesn't last long, usually 45 seconds to a minute.

If one of the adversaries survives he is the winner and he
dances a triumph dance over the corpse of the loser. The
winner's supporters join him in this dance. The supporters
of the loser claim his body, grieve over it, and then
resurrect him. Then the two dances merge into one celebration.

The pattern of ritual combat is classic: presentation and display; war

dance; combat; triumph dance and lament; resurrection; celebration. Its

combination of intensity, formality, personal commitment to aggression,

dance, and group celebration verges on true drama. Several times I've

used the exercise as the core of long improvisations. These can get

complicated--almost epic--involving wars between cities, the corona-

tions of rival kings, combat between culture heroes, trance dancing,

slavery, prolonged celebrations.

Ritual combat is either step three or step four work depending on how

richly the combat is embroidered with dramatic elements. Most step

four work--relating to others within narrative or other highly forma-

lized structures--are improvisations, scenes, open workshops, rehear-

sals, open rehearsals, performances, and scored roles. In step four

the special work of environmental theatre merges with the regular work

of traditional theatres. The aim of step four is to combine sponta-

neity, personalization, and group interaction with objective meanings,

ikonography, and a coherent mise-en-scene. Much step four work focuses

on specific projects.

Some of the most interesting step four work is improvisational, however,

In July 1971 I improvised an exercise with members of the Environmental

Theatre Workshop. Later, without planning to do so, I invented a version

of this exercise for an open workshop at the end of August. Here is a

description of the original exercise.

> Everyone lies on the floor in silence. Then people begin to
> rise one at a time and move in slow motion to the highest places
> in the space. As they move they say names very quietly; their
> own names, those of others in the workshop, people they know,
> or just names. They speak in slow motion so their words turn
> into sounds, are slurred, like talking under water or moaning.

> As each person arrives at the highest place--he chooses for
> himself what is highest for him--he freezes. When everyone is
> frozen the director says, "Take off your clothes and throw them
> down in slow motion." The clothes are taken off slowly, they
> are held out slowly, but of course they fall according to
> gravity. When the clothes are dropped the director says, "Those
> who are dressed go and pick up the clothes that have been thrown
> down and bring them to the center of the space."

Comment. Undressing is offered rather than required. The director must

be ready to take off from what is given him, but his directions ought

never be coercive. The director must feel free to say what he sees and

make whatever suggestions he feels--to follow his impulses which are

scenic. The performer must feel free to accept or reject what the direc-

tor suggests. In this way the work between them can become collaborative.

> When the clothes are brought to the center the people bringing
> them stop saying the names as soon as they put the clothes down.
> They freeze in whatever positions they are in when the clothes
> they are carrying touch the floor. When all the clothes are
> brought to the center the people in the high places stop calling
> names.

> Then silently, the people in the high places come down, moving
> in slow motion, and claim their clothes, dress, and find a safe
> place to lie down in and close their eyes.

> The people in the center rise from their frozen position, look
> at the ones who are lying down. The director says, "If you want
> to joint the ones lying down, take off your clothes, go to the
> person you want to join, put your clothes next to that person
> arranging your clothes in the position you want to be in, and
> return to the center, saying your name all the while. Then look
> back at yourself laying next to the one you wanted to join."

When the clothes have been placed and everyone has returned
to the center the director says, "Those lying down get up
and see if there are clothes next to you. If there are take
them to the person they belong to, saying his or her name
as you move in slow motion. If there are no clothes next to
you simply sit still and watch."

When all the clothes are returned and the people are all
dressed, allow the silence in the room to last for a long
time.

This exercise is an improvisation. All the director's words were made
up on the spot; the descriptions I wrote out several days after the
exercise was performed. The themes of the exercise are characteristic
themes in my work: of undressing, dressing, exchange of clothes; a
person's being-in-his-clothes and being-separate-from-his-clothes. I
believe that clothes are a deep, essentially human indicator of the
human condition; just as speech is characteristically human so are
clothes. I don't know exactly what I am working out for myself in an
exercise like the one just described, but I am deeply involved. In all
the steps of the work, but especially in step four, the director is
intimately involved, working through his obsessive themes along with the
performers. It is in this work that the risks of manipulation are most
apparent. The director is not a performer--he doesn't follow his own
impulses himself; he doesn't act out in a direct, graphic way what he is
feeling. Instead he directs, he makes scenic suggestions. These suggestions involve the performers in acting out the director's impulses. One
of the risks is that the performer will feel used, or even embarrassed
by what he's doing; another risk is that if the director does not make
suggestions that come from himself he will feel bottled up, angry, resentful. The long hours of work are a struggle to find that middle ground
where the director's impulses and the performer's impulses converge.
Necessarily this will be a small fraction of all the work tried. Most

of the time the performers work from their own impulses and the director watches, or reports what he sees, or helps remove blocks. But in
the midst of this the director makes his own suggestions which the performers accept when these suggestions are also suitable armatures for
the performers' own explorations.

Yet it isn't enough for the performer to be himself in a performance, or
to be the director's surrogate. Creativity starts from the self but
feeds into larger, collective structures. In theatre this larger struc-
ture is called action. During the last part of his life Stanislavski
turned to the problem of identifying action, of finding its actual uses
during rehearsals and performance. His "logic of physical actions" has
two parts--the details of the score and the connections among all these
details. Each detail is a fulfillment of its own needs--for example, a
halfback stretching his body so that it is horizontal to the football
field as the back makes an effort to catch the ball. Performers in
theatre strive for the same purity of detailed action, an absolute
identity between act and objective. But it is harder to get this kind
of purity in theatre because the physical task is complicated by psychological and mise-en-scenic aspects.

The ultimate problem of step four is to construct a score for each performer that makes sense to the audience (the connections of the logic
of physical action) while freeing each performer to pursue each action
for its own sake (the details of physical action). When this ideal state
is achieved--it never is--then each performer is wholly committed to
each moment of the performance, and the performance-as-a-unit will make
sense to the audience. The equivalent in football is a perfectly played

game before a stadium full of aficionados. Thus the theory may be correct, but its application is near impossible. Either the play makes sense but lacks conviction in performance, or the performers are really into it but the audience can't make heads or tails out of what's happening.

The best technique I know of to achieve a score made from the logic of physical actions is to relocate questions ordinarily asked intellectually so that they are asked of other parts of the body. For example, in Commune, when Clementine thrusts downward with her arm, hand, and fingers, pushing her fingers into Lizzie's belly at the climax of the Sharon Tate murder scene, the question for the performer is not "Why do I stab Lizzie?" but "How do I stab Lizzie?" The question of how is put to Clementine's arm, hand, and fingers; to her belly and shoulders; her face, teeth, and tongue. If each detail of the action is in place, if the connections between the details are strong and logical, then the whole action will be so together that any answer to the question of why is correct. (Or, to put it another way, knowing how makes knowing why unnecessary.) In fact, the answer to why will change from performance to performance, depending upon the immediate circumstances of the night. This changing response to why within a fixed set of actions is what is meant by the performer is free within his score. It is exactly as Grotowski says:

> The actor's score consists of the elements of human contact:
> "give and take." Take other people, confront them with one-
> self, one's own experiences and thoughts, and give a reply.
> In these somewhat intimate human encounters there is always
> this element of "give and take." The process is repeated,
> but always hic et nunc (here and now), that is to say, it is
> never quite the same.[12]

Here and now. A tension, confrontation, contact, exchange--between the

----
[12]
    Grotowski (1968), 212.

performer and the text; between the performer and his actions; between the performer and his partners; between the performer and the spectator; between the spectator and other spectators.

While working on Makbeth we couldn't find the actions of the play. We tried many different exercises but nothing worked. We knew what the actions were but we couldn't connect them to the body, or link them to each other. The poetry of the great soliliquies sounded extraneous. Peter Brook saw a performance and suggested an exercise. "Have the actors say the lines as fast as possible; have them recite the whole play in a half-hour. In this way the action underneath the psychology and poetry of the lines will be flushed out into the open." We tried the exercise-- it was not a cure-all--but it helped. Forced to give up tricks and superficial personalizations, without time to reflect on how beautiful the language was, the performers felt through the words to the action. (Feeling through is the body's equivalent to seeing through; it means to perceive an action through what was previously an opaque or deadening barrier.) Faced with a merciless task--saying the lines so fast they could not possibly think about what they were saying--things began to happen: shouts, laughter in unexpected places, fierce whispers; the actions became visible the way a landscape emerges from a lifting fog. The rehearsal began with people sitting in a large circle, but soon performers were up and moving. New relationships erupted as if from beneath a sea of words. Strong logical actions that defined the flow of whole scenes swept away the previous, too highly individualized treatments of text.

Unfortunately, the Group was unable to follow through on the exercise.

Terrible problems were shaking the Group to its foundations. Makbeth never achieved the rush, force, clarity, and beauty it had in that rehearsal. But I use Brook's exercise now when faced with a problem of not seeing the forest for the trees; or when things are bogged down in muddy detail; or when a text is encrusted with meaning.

Steadily in 1969 and 1970 the Group worked on the idea that feelings must flow freely through a set score of physical actions. This idea was put to a severe test during the spring of 1971 when the Group developed a new version of Commune. Originally Commune was composed by nine performers, an assistant director, and myself; we did the daily work. We were assisted by Paul Epstein and Jerry Rojo who worked with us occasionally. In the spring of 1971 we were looking for ways to free ourselves from relationships based on characters who were no longer in the play and performers who were no longer in the Group. Commune had to be remade for six performers. One afternoon I asked the performers to run through the play silently, playing every action but carefully avoiding dialog substitues such as nodding the head to signal yes. I wanted to test the actions for clarity, coherence, and wholeness. Whenever an action was unclear or unfulfilled the run-through was stopped and we worked on the detail.

Many actions were revealed as superfluous, others as unclear. Over the next few weeks much fat was cut from Commune, a very painful operation. For the first time a clear story was discovered at the core of Commune, and that story was embodied in a scenic rhythm. The work confirmed an opinion of Meyerhold's:

> Any dramatic work which is imbued with the quality of true theatricality is amenable to total schematization, even to the extent of temporarily removing the dialog with which the

> skeleton of the scenario is embellished. In this form,
> schematically and mimetically performed, a genuinely
> theatrical play can still stir the spectator, simply
> because the scenario is constructed from traditional,
> truly theatrical elements. [13]

The work of find the actions of a play fails when the director or per-

formers are impatient. Finding the action-score of a play takes hundreds,

maybe thousands of hours; most of this time is spent on solutions that

will ultimately be rejected. Discovering the logic of actions--and ruth-

lessly revising the mise-en-scene in terms of this logic--doesn't come

automatically, easily, or naturally. Tempers are short, the work gruel-

ling and repetitive. Many rehearsals go on for ours and end with no

measurable gains. The good-will of the company is tested.

Ultimately, I am not even certain that all changes in the direction of

clarity are for the best. I believe things can become too clear, too

easy and simpleminded. That art is best which incorporates irrelevancies,

lapses of logic, unresolvable tensions. Transcending mistakes does not

mean eliminating them. I am reminded of Kafka's short parable:

> Leopards break into the temple and drink to the dregs what
> is in the sacrificial pitchers; this is repeated over and
> over again; finally it can be calculated in advance and it
> becomes part of the ceremony.

From all this work each performer begins to find his role. A role is a

theatrical entity, not a psychological being. Great errors are made

made because performers and directors think of characters as people

rather than as dramatis personae: masks of dramatic action. A role

conforms to the logic of theatre, not the logic of any other life system

To think of a role as a person is like picnicking on a landscape painting.

---

[13] Meyerhold (1969, written in 1914), 150-151.

Theatrical logic is about <u>doing, showing, impersonating, singing, dancing,</u> <u>and playing</u>. These are the resources a performer calls on when preparing a role. Whatever "psychology" there is in a role is the psychology of the performer, his own personal being. The performer's contingent experiences confront the transcendent elements of the scored role. But it is not a simple confrontation of two self-contained entities. The score is made by the performer, out of the performer. He is his own material, he does not have the buffer of a media. Theatre is not an art that detaches itself from its creators at the point of completion; there is no way of exhibiting a performance without at the same time exhibiting the performers. And the experience of the performance for the audience are the innumerable and deep points of contact and interpenetration of performer and performance. These can be listed in only the most generalized way.

Performer	Performance
Person	Role
Self	Story, text, action
Immediate	Timeless
Continuous	Intermittent
Contingent	Transcendent
Here, now	Without time or place
Actual	Reactualization[14]
Unexpected	Already known
Experience	Metaphor or analogy
For the last time	Again and again

This way of working is different from that of the orthodox theatre. In orthodox theatre the actor wants to "get inside" the character; rehearsals concentrate on techniques that help the actor "lose himself in" the role. Devices such as emotional recall help the actor find in his own past analogs to the experiences of the character he is "portraying" so

---

[14] For a discussion of the concepts of "actual" and "reactualization" see Eliade (1965) and Schechner (1970a).

that <u>he can feel what the character is supposed to have felt</u>. In short,

the character is assumed to be a person and the actor's job is to become

that person. Environmental theatre does away with the "there are two

people" assumption. Rather there is the role and the person of the per-

former; both role and performer are plainly perceivable by the spectator.

<u>The feelings are those of the performer as stimulated by the actions of</u>

<u>the role at the moment of performance.</u>

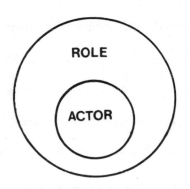

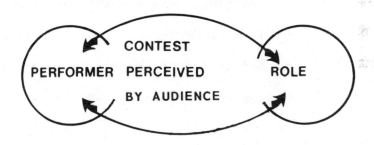

The orthodox actor vanishes inside his role. The environmental theatre

performer is in a perceivable relationship with the role. What the audi-

ence experiences is neither the performer nor the role but the relationship

between the two. This relationship is immediate, it exists only in the

here and now of performance. The performer doesn't try to mask his diffi-

culties; his way of dealing with the role is a major part of the interest

in the performance. The performer and the role are open to each other;

the performer uses "his role as if it were a surgeon's scalpel, to dissect

himself."[15] The reverse is also true: the performer's way of dealing with

the role illuminates it.

---

[15]
    Grotowski, <u>Towards a Poor Theatre</u> (1966), 206.

Most performances in environmental theatre do not achieve the purity of model 2. There remains degrees of orthodox acting. But I believe the model is attainable. It is a question of training performers, directors, and audiences to look at theatre not as a reflection or duplication of reality--as secondary realities; but as itself a primary kind of reality-- and then to interest people in the process of this performance reality.

Earlier I discussed verbophysical exercises. I want now to return to the subject of voice training. Voice work is intrinsic to every step of the training. While doing the association exercises performers are encouraged to make whatever sounds they wish. These sounds are not forced; they are a function of the physical work and of the associations. If a person unaccustomed to the way The Performance Group does the opening exercises were to listen to the first hour of a workshop, he would possibly think people were mad, in great pain, hysterical, in the throes of trance or orgasm. Every conceivable sound is made from laughing to screaming, sobbing, heavy breathing, moaning, gurgling, singing, shouting, reciting tongue-twisters, doing scales, etc.

The body shapes the voice; controls its intensity, volume, pitch, rhythm, duration, variety, and timbre. In the verbophysical exercises the performer does not think about what to say, he doesn't use the voice as the means of saying what he knows; he uses the voice as a <u>means of finding out what he is saying</u>. Using the voice need not be an expression of something more basic; using the voice is in itself an essential act. In this way new sounds, new songs, new languages are possible. Dialog is not limited to verbal language, or to the usual ways of using verbal languages. Sometimes by simply singing a song while doing a massive

exercise like the body roll uncovers new feelings, new ways of singing.
Sometimes performers "speak" with each other by breathing-and-dancing,
a form of unverbal, soundless language. The unverbal is the sonic counter-
part of the unconscious--a system of linguistic relationships not yet
formed into ordinary speech or song. Just as unconsciousness is continuously communicating with consciousness through daydreams and night dreams,
fantasies, and associations so the unverbal is always communicating with
the verbal through the "uhhs" and "ohhs" that accompany speech, breathing
sounds, body sounds like digestion, ringing in the ears, swallowing and
the noises polite people learn to ignore and suppress such as sudden
gasps, sobs, laughs, moans, shrieks. The association work helps the performer engage these sounds.

Once the voice is on its way to becoming free--once it no longer is the
servant of grammar, decorum, or literary poetry--it can make as well as
use language. Jerome Rothenberg in his dense, extremely rich preface to
the extraordinary book, Technicians of the Sacred, puts it this way:

> Poems are carried by the voice and sung or chanted in speci-
> fic situations. Under such circumstances, runs the easy
> answer, the "poem" would simply be the words-of-the-song.
> But a little later the question arises: what are the words
> and where do they begin and end? The translation, as
> printed, may show the "meaningful" element only, often no
> more than a single, isolated "line;" thus
>
> > A splinter of stone which is white (Bushman)
> > Semen white like the mist (Australian)
> > My-shining-horns (Chippewa: single word)
>
> but in practice the one "line" will likely be repeated until
> its burden has been exhausted. (Is it "single" then?) It
> may be altered phonetically and the words distorted from their
> "normal" forms. Vocables with no fixed meanings may be dis-
> torted from their "normal" forms. Vocables with no fixed
> meanings may be intercalated. All of these devices will be
> creating a greater and greater gap between the "meaningful"
> residue in the translation and what-was-actually-there. We
> will have a different "poem" depending where we catch the

movement, and we may start to ask: Is something within this work the "poem," or is everything?

Rothenberg answers his own question.

> The animal-body-rootedness of "primitive" poetry: recognition of a "physical" basis for the poem within a man's body--or as an act of the body and mind together, breath and/or spirit; in many cases too the direct and open handling of sexual imagery and (in the "events") of sexual activities as key factors in creation of the sacred; the poet as shaman, or primitive shaman as poet and seer through control of the means just stated: an open "visionary" situation prior to all system-making ("priesthood") in which the man creates through dream (image) and word (song), "that Reason may have ideas to build on." (W. Blake)[16]

It is not as difficult as it may seem to employ these concepts. Paul Epstein in working out the music for Makbeth approached sound topographically, as shapes rather than noises. For example, here is Epstein's text for Lady Makbeth's reading of Makbeth's famous letter.

LADY MAKBETH

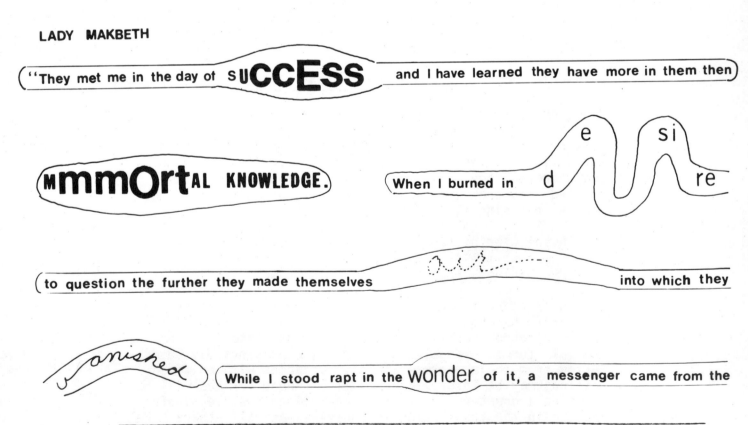

---

16 Rothenberg, ed. (1968), xxi-xxiv.

KINNNNNNNNG who hailed me ThANE OF CAWDOR...

and referred me to the coming of time with 'Hail KING that SHALT BE!' This have

I thought good to deliver thee my dearest partner of GREATNESS that thou mightest not lose

the dues of rejoicing by being ignorant of what is promised THEE. Lay it to thy heart, and farewell"

Epstein instructs the performers: "The graphic notation suggesting a heightened treatment of key words. The notation is both an approximate transcription/interpretation of things done in rehearsal and a score to be re-interpreted by the performer." The music of Makbeth was worked out collaboratively by Epstein and the performers within the environment at the Garage. (unlike the rest of the production, Epstein composed the music after the Group's return from Yugoslavia.) Epstein's piece, Concert for TPG is similarly a collaboration.[17]

---

[17] The second part of Concert, "Intersections 7" is printed in Scripts 2 (Volume 1, Number 2, December 1971), 62-70. There Epstein lays out the uses of space, the special notation for Concert, and rehearsal procedures.

Epstein writes of Makbeth:

> In much of the music of Makbeth the selection of text, on
> the basis of phonetic content as well as meaning, was a
> major part of the compositional task. "Text setting" came
> to mean literally that, placing pieces of text in relation
> to one another and to a context of scenic action. Duncan's
> funeral procession reverses itself to become Makbeth's coro-
> nation march. The transition is made musically as the
> funeral chants are replaced by miniature fanfares, the
> themes of the text fragments changing from purification and
> sleep to duty, honor, and the crown.
>
> (...)
>
> While Makbeth murders Duncan, the Dark Powers play out a
> scene of carousal that is parallel in its overall rhythmic
> shape. As Makbeth addresses the dagger and gradually moves
> towards action, the sounds of carousal are langorously
> seductive. Fragments of text resonate from one part of the
> scene to the other, and the sinuous phrases of inflected
> speech relate the carousal to Makbeth's lust for the crown.
> Both scenes climax at the same time, and the sound of the
> Dark Powers subsides into whispered phrases, the words
> chosen as much for their high sibilant content as for their
> sense.[18]

Makbeth is not an opera but an attempt to bring back into Western theatre

the sonic complexities, possibilities, ranges, and gut meanings of Asian

and "primitive" theatres where there is no hard division between music,

dance, and drama.

In some ways voice work transcends all of the four steps of performer

development. Voice work is at the same time the most sophisticated and

the most primitive element in training and performance. The voice is

identical to the breath--to the ancient notion of spirit, of life coming

from outside and possessing the body, or of man's essential inner life.[19]

---

[18] Epstein's two-part essay "Music and Theatre" lays out his aesthetics
and procedures. See Performance (Volume 1, numbers 2 and 4, 1972).
Epstein and I have worked together since the founding of the New
Orleans Group in 1965.

[19] The etymology of spirit is enlightening in this regard. Its Latin root
is spirare = to breathe, an onomatopoetic word. The Latin spiritus =
breath of life, life itself, soul--as well as a simple breath. Deriva-

Sound is to breath what gesture is to movement. People are always

breathing and therefore always making some ground noise; but sounding

the breath is signalling, and the range of signals and language is

incalculable. Levi-Strauss understands, as few people do, that questions

of vocalities touch the basic issues of human culture.

> (...) innumerable societies, both past and present, have
> conceived of the relation between the spoken language and
> singing or chanting as analogous to that between the con-
> tinuous and the intermittent. This is tantamount to say-
> ing that, within culture, singing or chanting differs
> from the spoken language as culture differs from nature;
> whether sun or not, the sacred discourse of my stands in
> the same contrast to profane discourse. Again, they are
> the acoustic equivalents of what actual masks represent
> on the plastic level (and, for this reason, in South
> America especially, they are associated, mentally and
> physically, with masks). [20]

Levi-Strauss sets up several transformational pairs of opposites:

continuous	intermittent
spoken	sung/chanted
profane	sacred
everyday	mythic
unadorned	masked
nature	culture

The first terms are the more inclusive, the matrices of the second. But

the second terms decay (in the musical sense) into the first. For example,

the face is usually unadorned, unmasked; but it is by painting the face,

dressing it, imitating it, distorting it that masks are made and worn;

and when the ceremony/celebration is over and the mask taken off and/or

destroyed, the face remains as before.

This same transformational exaltation characterizes performing. Out of

the daily tasks of training and rehearsing a performance arises, step by

---

tives include actions as diverse as conspire, inspire, perspire, and
transpire, and aspire.

[20]
    Levi-Strauss (1969b), 28.

step. It is performed for as many times as it is. Then it is dis-
mantled. A similar rhythm affects every performer. He arrives at the
theatre before show-time; prepares himself in some way for the peculiar
excitement of performing; performs; when the show is over he goes
through some procedures of coming down, restoring himself to a level
state again. The sequence warm-up, perform, cool-down is one action
unit. Performance itself is a heightened activity, an exalted state
that is intermittent, sacred, mythic, and masked. It is a special way
man has of singing.

The performer has qualities of the healer and the ecstatic. "The shaman
becomes the exemplar and model for all those who seek to acquire power.
The shaman is the man who knows and remembers, that is, who understands
the mysteries of life and death."[21] Few performers in the West achieve
this understanding, but the echoes and the aspirations remain. The work
of environmental theatre is to stir those coals, to raise the temperature
of theatre so that it will resume its critical importance.

> In treating his patient the shaman also offers his audience
> a performance. What is this performance? Risking a rash
> generalization on the basis of a few observations, we shall
> say that it always involves the shaman's enactment of the
> 'call,' or the initial crisis which brought him the revela-
> tion of his condition. But we must not be deceived by the
> word performance. The shaman does not limit himself to
> reproducing or miming certain events. He actually relives
> them in all their vividness, originality, and violence. And
> since he returns to his normal state at the end of the
> seance, we may say, borrowing a key term from psychoanalysis,
> that he abreacts. [22]

. . . .

The medicine man is a professional dealer in all kinds of anxie-

_____

[21]
    Eliade (1965), 102.
[22]
    Levi-Strauss (1963), 180-181.

ties connected with body destruction and primal scenes.
He has been initiated by having his own corruptible
intestines removed, i.e., by having undergone the punish-
ment for his body destruction fantasies, but also by over-
compensating this anxiety position. (...) The reparation
fantasies which always follow body destruction trends, are
introverted towards his own body, and then re-extroverted
towards his patients, whom he heals by stimulating their
own reparation fantasies. In healing them he heals
himself, by a permanent series of reparations.[23]

The performance is always about at least two things: the performer's

body and the story. The performance stimulates the audience to

react in their bodies to what's happening to the performer. The

stories are variations on a few basic themes, all of them involving

dismemberment and reparation. The performer says to the audience:

"Watch my insides being removed, watch as I spill my guts in front of

you, to you, for you; watch how I am healed." In watching, the audi-

ence participates in a cycle of conflict, agony, death, dismemberment,

and repair. True, the story being told may have great consequences and

meanings on the social level. But at the same time a profound visceral

experience is taking place, touching off deep reverberations in the

audience. During each performance the performer tries to find for

himself--and undergo in front of the audience--the process of birthing,

growing, opening up, spilling out, dying, and rebirthing. This is the

life-rhythm mystery of theatre, "live theatre." This is the kernel of

theatre's most personal experience, located at that place where art,

medicine, and religion intersect.

23
    Roheim (1969, written in 1945), 191.

63

References & Reading List

Notes: Dates are of editions I used, not of original publication. When I feel that the date of original publication is necessary, it is included in brackets following date of publication of edition I used.

Barba, Eugenio. 1965. "Theatre Laboratory 13 Rzedow," TDR (Volume 9, No. 3), 153-171

Castaneda, Carlos. 1968. The Teachings of Don Juan: A Yaqui Way of Knowledge. New York: Ballantine Books.
　　--1971. A Separate Reality. New York: Simon & Schuster.

Eliade, Mircea. 1965. Rites and Symbols of Initiation. New York: Harper Torchbooks.

Erikson, Erik H. 1959. Identity and the Life Cycle (Psychological Issues, Monograph 1). New York: International Universities Press.

Freud, Sigmund. 1958. On Creativity and the Unconscious. A collection of papers from all phases of Freud's career. New York: Harper & Row.
　　--1961 (1900). The Interpretation of Dreams, tr. by James Strachey. New York: John Wiley & Sons.

Goffman. Erving. 1959. The Presentation of Self in Everyday Life. Garden City: Doubleday Anchor Books.

Grotowski, Jerzy. 1968a. Towards a Poor Theatre. Holstebro: Odin Teatrets Forlag
　　--1968b. "Theatre & Ritual," tr. Malgorzata Ruska Munk in manuscript only. Original in Polish in Dialog magazine (1968, No. 9).
　　--1970. "Not Actor, Son of Man." article based on lectures at Brooklyn Academy in December 1969. Tr. George Reavey, in manuscript only.

Hall, E. T. 1959. The Silent Language. Garden City: Doubleday.
　　--1969. The Hidden Dimension. Garden City: Doubleday Anchor.

Kaplan, Donald M. 1968. "Theatre Architecture: A Derivation of the Primal Cavity," TDR (Vol. 12, No. 3), 105-116.

Kaprow, Allan. 1966. Assemblages, Environments, & Happenings. New York: Harry Abrams.

Kirby, Michael. 1965a. "The New Theatre," TDR (Vol. 10, No. 2), 23-43.
　　--1965b, with Richard Schechner, "An Interview with John Cage," TDR (Vol. 10, No. 2), 50-72.

Laing, R. D. 1950. The Divided Self. Chicago: Quadrangle Books.
　　--1962. The Self and Others. Chicago: Quadrangle Books.

Levi-Strauss, Claude. 1963. "The Sorcerer and His Magic," in Structural Anthropology, 167-185. New York: Basic Books.
　　--1966. The Savage Mind. Chicago: University of Chicago Press.
　　--1969. The Raw and the Cooked. New York: Harper & Row.

Living Theatre, The. 1969. "Paradise Now Notes," TDR, (Vol. 13, No. 3), 90-107.

Lorenz, Konrad. 1967. On Aggression. New York: Bantam Books.

Marcuse, Herbert. 1962. Eros & Civilization. New York: Vintage Books.

Meyerhold, Vsevolod Emilevich. 1969 (1902-1938). Meyerhold on Theatre, ed., tr., and with a critical commentary by Edward Braun. New York: Hill & Wang.

Performance Group, The. 1970. Dionysus in 69, ed. Richard Schechner. New York: Farrar, Straus, and Giroux.

Roheim, Geza. 1950. Psychoanalysis and Anthropology. New York: International Universities Press.
　　--1969 (1945). The Eternal Ones of the Dream. New York: International Universities Press.
　　--1971 (1943). The Origin and Function of Culture. New York: Anchor Books.

Schechner, Richard. 1969. Public Domain. New York: Bobbs-Merrill.
　　--1969a. "Containment is the Enemy," an interview with Judith Malina and Julian Beck, TDR (Vol. 13, No. 3), 24-44.
　　--1970. "Actuals: A Look into Performance Theory," in The Rarer Action, ed. Alan Cheuse and Richard Koffler, 97-135. New Brunswick: Rutgers University Press.

Slater, Philip. Microcosm. New York: John Wiley & Sons.

Winnicott, D. W. 1971. Playing and Reality. London: Tavistock Publications.

NOTES TO AN ACTOR

by Robert Benedetti

BECOMING

The theatre of the immediate future will be neither a theatre of seeming, nor one of being, it will be a theatre of Becoming; a theatre celebrating the unending flow of the present moment.

The actor of this theatre will perform thus, constantly realizing how his own great weight in existence lies like a stone on the thin membrane of his mortality; constantly defining himself through the dramatic act, which is itself an affirmation of the process of life.

In the beginning there was the act...we have enough words...we are looking for acts.
　　--Jerzy Grotowski in a talk at N.Y.U.

The theatre is a metaphor of life
in the sense that
real men exist by acting.
If one gives up acting
one commits a form of suicide.
So that acting is itself a metaphor;
you can see that.

Theatre investigates the conditions
which influence the committing of actions,
the process of action itself, and therefore
is continually involved with questions of
existence, since action is the means whereby
existence becomes self-defining.

All art is generated by a fundamental
esthetic conflict between form and
impulse, between the containment and
the release of energy, between something
coming to be and something ceasing to be.

Painting and sculpture are concerned
with this conflict as it is manifested
in line, mass, texture, color, figure
and ground. Music realizes it in tonality,
silence, and time. Drama realizes it in
the lives of men.

Each play expresses the process of
becoming, the fundamental esthetic
conflict, in some specific way so as to
illuminate the human condition.   Each
play focuses upon some specific aspect of
man's attempt to deal with the flow of
time.

The deepest vitality of the play flows
from this profound stratum. Dramatic
action, therefore, must touch an ancient
part of us, must deal with survival--that
is, with existence through time.

The sequence of events in a play, its
plot, are a form given to this fundamental
vitality. So are the play's characters and
language. Aristotle saw this, though as an
almost metaphysical (or at least merely
esthetic) idea, rather than as we see it
today, as a physical and spiritual reality.

The most accessible window
May not give the best view.
The truest view
Can never be seen
From only one window.

66

Drama must occur in the present
for only the present is always
and the only
true point of suspense.

The present is
a process of formation

By which form is given
to the limitless energy of the future

And the lifeless hulks of the known
drift into memory.

Drama is concerned with man's influence on
and subjectivity to
this process of becoming.

Truth, for an actor, cannot exist a priori or even continue existing the moment after it comes to be; the actor's truth is in the act of unfolding the infinite present, in showing the inherent drama of our existence.

The sense of drama derives from the shaping of experience along the continuum of the present, the realization that we are in a state of continual expectation and that human interaction and emotion are mechanism and manifestations of our incessant and dramatic encounter with the next moment.

A performance is an organism which,

like any organism,

is continuously dying and being reborn.

It may pass a crisis

when the dying overtakes the borning

as it is said we all do.

67

All plays occur in the present, the
events happening not "as if" but
actually "before our eyes." The tone
of each play is much determined by the
way it orients itself to the flow of
time; standing in the present it may
either greet the future or honor the
past.

In the comedic posture man eagerly
embraces the oncoming moment, saying
his incessant "hello."
Tragedy lingers at the threshold of
the past and lets us say our incessant
"goodbye."

Tragedy is autumn passing into winter.
Goodbye.

Comedy is spring and the promise of
summer. Hello.

We stand in the present and our
view backward is as distorted as
our view forward is conjectural.
The telling of the future is,
like the telling of the past, an
act of interpretation, a selection
of alternatives. Unlike the
social or political historian,
the artist finds the future more
attractive than the past; the
past has form, its circumstances are
essentially beyond control. The
past can be known but not met. But
the future is suspenseful; it can
be met but not known. Creative
happiness comes from man's participation, through his art, in the meeting
of the future, in his destiny. In
his art, man can truly "get on with
it."

The real distinction between the "establishment" theatre and the avant-garde today is the difference between product and process. The commercial product is just that, a product, over, finished, dead.

It has ceased to change in any essential way, and in this universe arrested change is eventual death. Now matter how long the rewrites go on (from Burrows to Albee to Chance), no matter how many changes are made during previews, the essential life of it was over somewhere back in the producer's office.

The commercial product strives to give the impression that the actor is immortal, even plasticized, and that even if he should crack and go bad, don't worry, we have 420 other actors waiting for the part with no noticeable change in the performance. Most of the actors working steadily in New York are replacements in long runs. They play the part of the actor who played the part of the actor who "created" the role.

By the time it gets to us it cannot hurt us. The actor's mortality, his spark of the vanished instant, has been captured and neutralized; he dies/lives in a life/death before us.

The avant-garde, the best of it, the part which isn't establishment theatre hiding under a foundation grant or academic robe, is a theatre of process. Whatever it may be telling you, it is also saying, "whoops, there it goes, that will never happen again."

And hopefully it helps you to realize that you will never happen again; whoops, there you go.

The theatrical experience must be one
of process because it is the blending of the
life-forces of a small, temporary tribe moving
through time, dying and being reborn at each
moment.

What is therefore really unique and trans-
cendant about the theatre is that the actor
might drop dead.

THE MASK OF ACTIONS

The mechanism of the actor's process of
self-definition and of the dramatic event itself is a mask of actions; this
concept of a mask of actions is replacing the traditional idea of character
in drama.

The realistic theatre was obsessed with character; the theatre of the
next half-century will likely return it's focus, as most avant-garde groups
did in the 60's, to doings. Character, as an element of drama, will more and
more take its rightful place as the means by which action is specified and
qualified. This sense of character as the agency which performs action is
as old as Aristotle, but the future theatre will likely take the concept
to an extreme, deriving character entirely from agency. This is one reason
why athleticism, the physical virtuosity of the actor, will be more and more
important; character will more and more be a function of committing a pattern
of activity and plays will be more a sculpturing of events in time and space.

Theatre--through the actor's technique, his art in which the living organism strives for higher motives--provides an opportunity for what could be called integration, the discarding of masks, the revealing of the real substance: a totality of physical and mental reactions. Here we can see the theatre's therapeutic function for people in our present day civilization. It is true that the actor accomplishes this act, but he can only do so through an encounter with the spectator --intimately, visibly, not hiding behind a cameraman, wardrobe mistress, stage designer or make-up girl-- in direct confrontation with him, and somehow "instead of" him. The actor's act--discarding half measures, revealing, opening up, emerging from himself as opposed to closing up--is an invitation to the spectator...This act, paradoxical and borderline, we call a total act. In our opinion it epitomizes the actor's deepest calling.

--Jerzy Grotowski,
Towards a Poor Theatre

The theatre like the plague is a crisis which is resolved by death or cure. And the plague is a superior disease because it is a total crisis after which nothing remains except death or an extreme purification. Similarly, the theatre is a disease because it is the supreme equilibrium which cannot be achieved without destruction. It invites the mind to share a delirium which exalts its energies; and we can see, to conclude, that from the human point of view, the action of theatre, like that of plague, is beneficial, for, impelling men to see themselves as they are, it causes the mask to fall, reveals the lie, the slackness, baseness, and hypocrisy of our world; it shakes off the asphyxiating inertia of matter which invades even the clearest testimony of the senses; and in revealing to collectivities of men their dark power, their hidden force, it invites them to take, in the face of destiny, a superior and heroic attitude they would never have assumed without it.

--Antonin Artaud,
The Theatre and Its Double

Several studies on acting have been organized around the idea of _masks_. The central question is whether the character which the actor protrays is a mask which he only wears, or whether (or to what degree) it becomes his own face.

The principal of the mask must be understood in a very broad way: a mask, or the principle of maskness, is _any mechanism or behavior which is designed to project a sense of the self._

Persona is the word for mask, and it's the word from which we derive the word _personality_. Personality is a mask, a pattern of behavior whereby we present a sense of ourselves to our society.

Theatre is, in fact, based upon this everyday life-principle. We, in real life, perform sets of actions which become a mask presented to others, upon which our social audience projects a sense of authentic "self" which they tend to credit to the person performing those actions. If I convince you that I am a certain way, it is not necessarily because I am that way, but because I have performed my mas of actions successfully.

First, character. In our society the character one performs and one's self are somewhat equated, and this self-as-character is usually seen as something housed within the body of its possessor, especially the upper parts thereof, being a nodule, somehow, in the psychobiology of person-ality. (Here, however) the per-formed self was seen as some kind of image, usually creditable, which the individual on stage and in character effectively attempts to induce others to hold in re-gard to him. While this image is entertained concerning the individual, so that a self is imputed to him, this self itself does not derive from its possessor, but from the whole scene of his action, being generated by that attribute of local events which renders them interpretable by witnesses. A correctly staged and performed scene leads the audience to impute a self to a performed character, but this imputation--this self--is a pro-duct of a scene that comes off, and is not a cause of it. The self, then, as a performed character, is not an organic thing that has a specific loca-tion, whose fundamental fate is to be born, to mature, and to die; it is a dramatic effect arising diffusely from a scene that is presented, and the charac-teristic issue, the crucial con-cern, is whether it will be credited or discredited.

--Erving Goffman,
The Presentation of Self
in Everyday Life

The authentic self is a process, not a thing, it's not "here I am, I give my-self to you," it is the act of being. Our sense of self is not even a function of our physical existence: other physical things do not, so far as we know, have a sense of themselves. The self of which we are aware is not a thing at all; it is a living process, primarily a process of interaction between us and our environ-ment.

It is my actions which invite your sense of my authenticity, your sense of my self, not the authenticity of the performer who lies behind those actions. We know this because sometimes even our own social performances, performances which we've rehearsed all our lives, don't work. We've all experienced that horrible sense of alienation, that horrible sense of beginning to wonder who we are in such moments. This is because we not only present our mask of actions to others, but we also derive much of our own sense of identity from our own performances; both from the affirmation of our audience and from being our own audience. When the performance is unsuccessful, we become unsure of who we are. We do, that is, so long as we are seeking a state of being, a sense of our own self as a "thing," rather than of ourselves as a dynamic process of interaction between our organism and our environment through our actions and reactions.

Most avant-garde theatre is dedicated to providing us therapy from this delusion of the self as a "thing," forcing us instead to confront our own mortality, our own inescapable participation in the flow of the present. That is, to recognize our habitual mask of action as not being necessarily our authentic self.

> ...the primal phenomenon of
> duality, the incarnate
> presence of that which is
> remote, the shattering en-
> counter with the irrevocable,
> the fraternal confluence of
> life and death.
>
> This duality has its
> symbol in the mask.
>
> The whole splendor of
> that which has been submerged
> draws imperatively near at
> the same time that it is
> lost in eternity. The wearer
> of the mask is seized by the
> sublimity and dignity of
> those who are no more. He
> is himself and yet someone
> else. Madness has touched
> him--something of the mystery
> of the mad god, something
> of the spirit of the dual
> being who lives in the mask
> and whose most recent descen-
> dant is the actor.
> --Walter Otto,
> _Dionysis: Myth and Cult_

Even if I'm not wearing a literal, concrete mask, but instead have adopted the mask of actions, postures, and sounds which is, for example, Falstaff, you still have some glimmer of my own identity lurking behind that mask of action which is Falstaff.

Realistic acting worked against that tension; it tried to convince you that the performer and character being performed were one and the same. I think one of the sources of artistic tension and richness which realism tended to lack was exactly this sense of dual existence.

The man who wears the mask of Dionysis participates in the god, he becomes the god in a very special way, because he is at the same time also himself. The god is forever, the god is infinite in space and time; man is limited in space and time, but the wearer of the mask participates in infinity. And I'm convinced that one of the major reasons that people become actors is because of their desire to participate in the infinite.

It is possible, then, to be presenting yourself quite "honestly," but to have that presentation misinterpreted, so that people have a mistaken sense of you. At the same time, it's possible (and usual) to project a somewhat distorted sense of yourself which is believed to be authentic.

This distinction between the performer and the mask of action which he performs is essential to theatre. Many of the tensions which give theatre its estheticism, richness, and complexity, spring from the fact that the performer has a different mode of existence than the mask of actions which he performs. Not just the way he looks and sounds, but what he does.

The actor's reality is in principle therefore the same as our everyday social reality: a pattern of actions and reactions with others and the total environment which define the sense of self as they are performed.

The oriental theatre has manisfested this principle of character derived from action in one way; there are other ways. In the oriental theatre many patterns of gesture have certain connotation, a certain association and meaning which is known to the audience by convention. The character of the person committing the action has less impact on the action than in the western theatre, since the action has, by convention, stable meanings of its own. The western theatre does not have conventions in this way, nor is it likely to have. It is much more a theatre of contexts within which actions must be interpreted and our theatre manipulates subtleties of context much more than does the oriental theatre.

In real life we often manipulate our environment, creating a context within which our actions can be interpreted in the best light. Have you ever caught yourself putting the books you would like people to know you read into prominent places on your shelf? In this way things can become part of our character.

So too on the stage we are concerned not only with the creation of a performance which is a set of actions, but also with the creation of the context within which those actions are to be interpreted. In fact, the context is often more important to us than our individual activity: the most important part of our stage context is the other actors, and they share a mutual obligation to provide a proper context for each other's actions. Your job as an actor is not simply to perform your own actions but also to participate in all actions by all characters.

From this we know that our tradition of an actor playing his own character is false, that, in truth, all actors must perform all characters, that <u>we create each other on the stage</u> through the interaction of our masks of actions within the overall action of the play.

Actors often use images of animals, movie stars, or ideal "models" which they hold in their minds and which encourage in them responses appropriate to the character. Some actors confuse these images with the character itself, as we sometimes confuse our idea of ourselves with ourselves; but the images have nothing to do with the character or actor's self; they are mechanisms which may help to develop the mask of actions of the performance, but it is the performance itself which creates the character and the actor.

We know that kinetic and kinesthetic deprivation in infancy inhibits personality development. The social persona is rehearsed in our first years largely through kinetic experience; it stands to reason that the dramatic persona is best rehearsed in the same way. Every actor knows that it doesn't mean a thing until we get it up on its feet. It is only then, with script out of hand, in spatial and dynamic relationship with our partners and our environment, experiencing the transference of energy through our mutual pursuit of dramatic action that our role really begins to grow. Even Stanislavski, that great creator of "psycho-technique," was led in his last work to an emphasis on physical images and experience as the best inroads to the actor's total organism, and hence his unconscious as well.

Moreover, the dramatic persona itself (we can't really go on speaking of "character" nowadays) is not only communicated to an audience through sensation but may actually be said to consist of a mask of actions (vocalization is also a muscular gesture), a pattern of organismic activity upon which the audience is led to project a full sense of identity: as a pattern of organismic behavior in which both audience and actor participate and which, as an essentially kinetic experience, is capable of generating a profound impact on the personality of both.

It is an idea fundamental to Artaud and Grotowski, but which needn't necessarily lead one in their directions.

From all this it seems an inescapable conclusion that movement training in the broadest sense (and thus encompassing vocal training) is the most important single aspect of a young actor's development. Every serious training program that I know of has come or is coming to this realization.

The idea of mask must not be restricted to the face alone. Even our reading of facial expression in real life is much determined by the condition of the entire body. This is why an actual mask can so easily appear to change its expression. The masks of the Noh drama are designed to be expressionless so that they are free to receive the audience's projection of apparent changes in expression guided by the play's context and the activity of the wearer's entire body. The mime paints his face an expressionless white for the same reason. Actor's must learn how, in this way, less is more; the performance must always leave room for the audience's contribution.

The mask of actions cannot be fully developed until the actor has found the specific playable action or point or reaction in each moment, expressed simply and actively. This should not be described in words but rather in experience.

Many intelligent students suspect this singular sense of the action of being an oversimplification of the interpretive subtleties and complexities of the moment; but the actor's organism demands a specific point of concentration which must be simple.

This point of concentration will mobilize his entire organism, if his preparation is thorough, and will excite the richness and subtlety of response which will create the full moment in the doing of it.

Like the baseball player who must, as he bats, free his mind of all considerations except hitting the ball, but whose focused action mobilizes months of self-conscious rehearsal on stance, weight shift, swing, grip, and so forth.

Since acting is becoming through doing, the actor's task is as much athletic as it is interpretive.

The past of a character is of far less use to an actor than is the character's future.

A character's future is expressed, in the present, through intention or reaction. The actor touches the character's future by surrendering (or rather joining) to the character's intention. From this intention, which has now become the actor's intention, comes the energy which drives the actor/character into the future.

The actor struggles to give form to this pattern of energy moving ahead into time through his technique. The result of his struggle is the mask of actions which confronts the audience.

THE ACTOR

This is the eternal origin of art that a human being confronts a form that wants to become a work through him. Not a figment of his soul but something that appears to the soul and demands the soul's creative power. What is required is a deed that a man does with his whole being: if he commits it and speaks with his being to the form that appears, then the creative power is released and the work comes into being.

The deed involves a sacrifice and a risk. The sacrifice: infinite possibility is surrendered on the altar of the form...The risk: the basic work can only be spoken with one's whole being; whoever commits himself may not hold back part of himself...it is imperious: if I do not serve it properly, it breaks, or it breaks me.

--Martin Buber, I and Thou

A role is a journey

And at any moment

You can only be at that one point

To which your steps

Have led.

There are, in the mountain tundra, vast heaps of talus, jumbled expanses of boulders of all sizes and shapes, which you must sometimes cross. They lie threatening you like the tumultuous boilings of a gigantic caldron frozen in stone.

You may cross in one of four ways:

--as most do, climbing painfully with hands as much as feet like some scuttling anachronism;

--as many do, trying to select a pathway through the stones but continuously discovering that as their point of view shifts, the planned pathway is impossible.

--as a few do, leaping to the top of a boulder and discovering a plane of points, like tiny mountain peaks poking through clouds, or islands from a sea, which it is possible to cross by leaping from point to point;

--as the artist must, by joining the rock, by finding at each instant only the next step and trusting the flow of his own activity to carry him to his goal.

Crossing the talus, find the next stepping place no matter its apparent direction and eventually the way will be found. As you begin to flow with the rock and its space you begin to run.

Actors must at some time learn to be more moved than moving. When we open ourselves to the energies of the play and let them flow through us, we discover that every good play is itself a source of vitality. The good actor doesn't make things happen, he lets things happen and joins them.

We often assume that playwrights write for audiences--but the actor must realize that good playwrights always write for actors.

Those of us who have learned a foreign language later in life, when our thoughts had been firmly fixed in English, realize that it did something for our thinking in English. Being forced to learn how to translate gave us a sense of ideas that we had never had before, and made us realize that all of us are translating all the time, even if we speak only one language. An idea pre-exists its verbal expression, and to find the proper mode of expression for an idea is an act of translation.

Acting stands very much in that relationship to real life. Acting on the stage is a translation of real patterns that exist in everyday life into the forms demanded by public

81

performance and by the theatre itself at our point in time. The theatre becomes the language into which we are translating the truths from real life. In order to translate well, one must know both languages thoroughly. We must understand life and we must also understand the theatre, which is the language into which we are translating.

The Zen Buddhist believes that the gardener's job is to extend nature in the direction in which it is already going. That is what we must do when we translate our truths from everyday life into the language of the theatre. We must use the theatre in such a way as to take those truths from life and expand them in the theatre in the direction in which they are already going.

A sign of the understanding of things by the new actors is the great stillness at the center which so many of them bring to their work; time was when such a stillness was found only in older actors, in your Scofields and your Redgraves, and especially in very old actors, in the Gielguds and the Munis. It is a source of great strength and freedom of imagination, this stillness at the center. It comes from understanding things. It will make the theatre an even more valuable place in the years to come, a place where once again all may dip into the pool, and touch the stillness.

In any case, the actor must see the **vital** center
of his play. It is not in the events, nor in the passions,
nor in the characters, but in a total, physical and spiritual
(which come to be one) participation in the action of the
drama, understood in the deepest possible way within the
race experience. The actor participates in his action as
the Yogi participates in the essential energy from which
the world of form derives.

"Remember that in an etude the aim is always
action, not emotion. Etudes are given for
the sole purpose of enabling emotion to
arise from action. These are not my words,
they're Stanislavsky's."
                                --Eugene Vakhtangov

The central condition for the actor

who is in a state of becoming through

doing is

KINETIC ACCORD

A theatre of Becoming requires a reversal of the way most actors have been
taught to work for the past half century. They've been taught to work from
character to actions, to be a character rather than to become it.

Picasso has a roomful of paintings which no one else has ever seen. Some aren't finished, some aren't good enough but too good to destroy, and many are simply <u>his</u>.

Actors have such rooms in their minds full of unfinished performances and performances which are simply their own private property.

It is important to the actor, like the painter, to say to something which he has made, "I love you."

The essential thing
is to find yourself
(growing younger)
in your work

A MANTRA:

The actor cares

But not for himself

The actor shares

But does not exhibit

The actor loves

But does not court

The actor receives

But does not take

The actor's joy

Is in the truth.

See now who he is

But what he has made.

Jim has given himself to acting completely; it was a deliberate choice. Already he has begun to learn the everyday things that start to accumulate, building the mound of wisdom, of artistry. No monumental revelations, but chips and sweepings that begin to fill the corners of the mind until he will sit, simply, quietly, a man of the theatre, sure that he's never really done his best. But the actor has early learned to love himself enough to forgive himself, moment by moment, for the inevitable incompleteness of his art. This Jim has already learned.

84

The greatest sickness of our theatre

is that so few of our actors have an appetite

for the truth. We have systematically

created a pantheon of false truths to which

the majority of our actors aspire, the

greatest of which is reputation.

Even the truths given the theatre by

its finest minds are quickly veneered by

reputation until they lose their power to

disturb us and to generate our quest for

the beautiful. As James Agee says, "the

weak in courage are strong in cunning,

and one by one you have captured, and have

distilled of your deliverers the most

ruinous of all your poisons... Official

acceptance is the one unmistakable symptom

that salvation is beaten again."

Sadly, **many** teachers whose perceptions become "recognized" lose much of their

potency, since their leadership is then sought for wrong reasons, and their

thoughts accepted as rote methodology rather than as the living, often

contradictory, and agonized struggle with fundamental esthetic principles

which they are.

To see that this is true you need only realize how much of Stanislavski's

work has been "frozen" at some particular point of its development and is

now taught as completed system. The overall direction of his entire life's

search is little taken into account. As a result we fail to continue his work

and instead have attempted to capture and endlessly repeat it. Thus we lose

the potency of his perceptions which should be signposts in the path of our

own search.

Beginning with Artaud in the thirties, there has been a feeling that theatre ought to get out from under the "dictatorship of speech." This anti-verbal feeling comes from a misunderstanding of the function and nature of language in life, which itself reflects one of the limitations of our culture.

We are bombarded by anonymous voices from the media and it often seems that the act of speech has ceased to be a physical and totally expressive act. We live in an age of the plastic voice. It has become a cultural norm, and in order to reproduce it in ourselves and our children we begin to develop, unconsciously, inhibitions of the expressive processes of the body which produce speech. Rather than regard speech as an enemy to theatre, it should be one of the mission of the theatre to restore to our culture a sense of the real expressiveness and force of language.

Speech forms a kind of pointing, and more specifically, a kind of grasping. You can see this in babies; at a certain age they can reach out and grasp an object physically; at some point they discover that the voice can reach further than the arm. The word or sound becomes a way to possess, a kind of long distance tasting. Language from the beginning has this physical basis as a way of extending the power of oneself through space. This sense of language as a force with which we can sculpt the space of the stage, with which we can create textures in the space of the stage, with which we can exert a real, physical influence on our environment, must be restored to the stage.

An actor's weight is
His principal reality.
He feels it
In the soles of his feet,
In every inclination,
Rotation,
Change in altitude
In every motion
At every moment.
There is no relationship
Where weight is not given
And taken.

Western theatre operates on a principal of Western culture, that when you can do a thing better, you do it faster; Classical Eastern theatre believes that when you can do a thing better, you do it slower. Both/neither are complete; as you do a thing better you improve your own (and your audience's) spiritual realization of the particular tempo of the thing itself.

Freedom of conception for the actor must include free disposition of his weight. Karate, tumbling, Tai Chi and the rest can liberate the actor by extending his range of choice. Imagine yourself onstage, knowing that you could, if you chose, leap into the air and flip over. This possibility so alters your range of choice that hosts of new possibilities, physical and spiritual, come easily within view.

Karate, Tai Chi, the rest, are all excellent disciplines for the

actor, at least until our theatre is sufficiently developed to make

its own unique demands upon us. Beware of Yoga, however, which, in

its passivity and self-relatedness, may lead one away from theatre.

Hatha-Yoga as a purely physical discipline is valuable.

Gardening is an excellent discipline

for the actor's spirit

and conception.

An exercise:

grow one plant from seed,

to root

to stem

to branch

to leaf

to flower

to autumn

to death/birth

to seed.

Identify each in the growth

of your next role.

For those who cannot garden

(should theatre happen where one cannot?)

WALK.

Long walks,

The labor of walking purges the body,   at first with a destination;

the rhythm of walking purges the soul.   gradually, without.

--Colin Fletcher

Drama was in the beginning a celebration at least in part of

the rhythm of the land.

There is for us

a desperate need to feel it again.

88

In comedy

the moment surrenders

to the actor;

In tragedy

the actor must surrender

to the moment.

COMEDY: Director sees impulse, gives the actor a sense of

the direction along which the impulse may be extended.

Or director may excite the creation of the impulse

or better, or impulses between actors.

TRAGEDY: Director puts the actor in touch with the material,

gives him a mode of perception

whereby the necessity of the moment may assert itself.

Thus comedy celebrates the ascendency of man over time

and tragedy his surrender to it.

Ripeness.

Comedy the promise of spring

Tragedy the ripeness of autumn.

Ripeness.

As the ocean waves, so the universe peoples.
--Alan Watts

As the plant grows, so grows man;

comedy the sowing,

tragedy the reaping.

Ripeness.

The **actor** has always known this in the rhythms of comedy

and tragedy,

in the direction of the force that drives through each.

The root of the matter is the way in which we feel and conceive ourselves as human beings, our sensation of being alive, of individual existence and identity. We suffer from a hallucination, from a false and distorted sensation of our own existence as living organisms. Most of us have the sensation that "I myself" is a separate center of feeling and action, living inside and bounded by the physical body--a center which "confronts" an "external" world of people and things, making contact through the senses with a universe both alien and strange. Everyday figures of speech reflect this illusion. "I came into this world." "You must face reality." "The conquest of nature."

This feeling of being **lonely** and very temporary visitors in the universe is in flat contradiction to everything known about man (and all other living organisms) in the sciences. We do not "come into" this world; we come out of it, as leaves from a tree. As the ocean "waves" the universe "peoples." Every individual is an expression of the whole realm of nature, a unique action of the total universe. This fact is rarely, if ever, **experienced** by most individuals. Even those who know it to be true in theory do not sense or feel it, but continue to be aware of themselves as isolated "egos" inside bags of skin.

--Alan Watts, <u>The Book</u>

There are many actors

for whom images and remembrances

of performance

are more acute than

performance itself.

Question to Mr. Strassberg:

Why is a seventy-five year old actor

the best fourteen year old

in the Chinese Opera?

Can he have

Public Solitude?

Answer to myself:

He can,

in his theatre,

but I can't,

in yours.

We are suggesting here a way of looking at the actor's function; we are not developing a system in the way that Stanislavski spoke of his "system." Techniques of analysis and systems of criticism are useful only insofar as they help to explore, extend, and clarify our esthetic responses; they can never be a substitute for esthetic response. When they begin to determine or predispose esthetic response they must be destroyed. The same thing applies to an educational situation. The moment you let any teacher's system or way of seeing things begin to replace your own, that's now education in any sense of the word whatsoever. Anything that can be taught on that basis is really not worth learning.

When thinking about your work and the work of your teachers remember that the real effect of your training will never be immediately apparent, nor will you be able to recognize or evaluate those deepest effects for some time. This is why firm trust in your teachers is indispensible.

The director's purpose is to create a condition which leads another (the actor) to a new experience...a thousand times it won't work, but once it will-- and that once is essential.

--Jerzy Grotowski in a talk at N.Y.U.

The director must not use his actors

    as instruments to make

    his own music,

but orchestrate theirs

    until it becomes one song

    which he can then

    share in singing.

The director is the magnifying lens

    through which the actor's impulse shines;

The director is the resonator

    which lends depth to the actor's music.

Work done in the mountains

    or in the forest

Is different than city work.

An actor, open as he must be to his place,

    his fellows,

Is played by his world

    like a violin.

The city plucks you

    and bows harshly

producing perhaps greater volume

and often a vivid melody,

But the mountains play you deep

    and long

    in sustained chords

    and with a truer song.   Recycle this book.

Style is a mode of perception,

The **pathway** from intention to execution,

The synthesis of form and material.

Performance in the theatre of becoming is, in fact, not an act of presentation at all: it is really the excitation and reception of projections from the audience within a carefully controlled context. In this theatre the actor's job is neither to seem, nor to be, nor to present; it is to excite through action and then to serve as host and guide for the resulting responses. It is this function that the actor shares with the priest.

Observe your reaction at a movie or play. Notice how, unaware, you identify with the characters. With which characters? Are there characters with whom you find it hard to identify?

Ability to evoke such identifications from the audience is crucial to an art-work's success in establishing its "reality" --that is to say, its illusion of reality. Popularity of the work stems largely from this. Yet works of art which accomplish only this have no great value, for it is a cheap experience (in no sense a re-creation) to drain off emotions by habitual channels, whether real or fantasied. An art-experience is worth your while only if it leads you to a difficult identification, some possibility in yourself different from what is customary in action or wish--a larger vision or a subtler analysis. Furthermore, since from the standpoint of the serious artist, the handling, style and technique is of highest importance, remember that you cannot grasp this by simply sinking into the characters but only by concentrating on how they are being created. As you become aware of the style along with your awareness of the characters and plot, you will be identifying with the artist and will share something of his joy of creation.
                --Frederick Perls, Ralph Hefferline,
                  and Paul Goodman, Gestalt Therapy.

93

"Illusion," as it was once called in
the theatre, is a matter of encouraging
the audience to re-interpret their (and
our) reality. The strength of the rein-
terpretation depends entirely on the
strength and fullness of our performance
reality.

The performance reality is one of
real organisms in real space, expressing
real energies in real conflict.

The actor who ignores performance
reality is lost.

Our roles in real life are in many ways as set as a dramatic
performance, and the range of choices available to the actor in his role are as
great as those offered to him by his social role.

Within any form, no matter how narrow, there exists an infinity of choice.
As the specific demands of the form increase (as in "stylized" performance) the
scale of choice decreases, but the range of choice does not.

Becoming in all kinds of performance is dependent on realizing and
experiencing this, and participating fully in the act of choice-making on the largest
scale of choice made available by the form.

A single breath offers such an infinity of possibilities.

The man on the airplane is a nuero-chemist. He reveals that the oldest part of the brain, in its stem in the hollow at the top of the neck, is concerned with homeothermic responses--our impulse to find comfortable temperatures, and thus a major instrument of racial survival. The esthetic response, we agree, ought to touch such a deep and ancient part of us; but have we ever fiddled with the temperatures of our theatres to do it? We are still seeking the optimum comfort in our art; when will we finally begin to disorder the very apparatus of survival for the sake of our art? We agree, but he is a 50 year-old Jew and he reminds me that Hitler succeeded thus in his art. But our art is not Hitler's; it is not an art of control and manipulation of response, of thought, I say. The actor-fascist who enjoys manipulating his audience's minds is being replaced by a magician, by a giver of truth and delight. He hopes so. We fly on.

FILLING THE GAPS IN THE STANISLAVSKI SYSTEM

by William Jaeger

One of the shortcomings of Stanislavski's System is that it lacks what
we might call operational referents; the classification and description
of such loosely formulated constructs as "the Magic If," "sense memory"
and "Imagination" lack a precision and are ultimately interpreted
according to each actor's personal taste. Lacking any objective standards
for the interpretation of the artist's language, the actor must inevi-
tably fall back on his own conception of the character. And how different the Richard the Thirds in a prison production from a women's club
production--and how different either of them from a Broadway production!

Language must be about something. If it weren't, we'd have no grounds
for complaint when a ham actor virtually trills Hamlet into a walking
absurdity, or broods Richard III into a Hamlet. An actor who maintains
that he is simply dealing with his subjective experience, which cannot
be encompassed in a descriptive system, is essentially putting himself

on stage as a character in his own right; he cancels the art he supposedly is trying to interpret.

We assume that even if their meanings do not remain constant over a period of generations a word today will mean roughly the same thing to you as it does to me. If it doesn't, we simply are not communicating. And though the problem of word variability is, in a sense, simplified for the playwright whose lines do not vary in form, his difficulties in communicating the text and subtext of his work are formidable since his meaning, or plot sense, must be understood and interpreted first by his actors and only then by his prime communicants, his audience.

And since words, attached to a human being, enter the field of dynamic movement, of life, we are faced with a second problem. How can we be reasonably sure that an actor's gestures, his non-verbal communication, will complement what he is saying? that they will, in short, have the same operational referents as what he is saying (and what, also, the playwright is trying to communicate through the actor)? The actor's previous experience is the guiding factor in his perception of any symbol system. Lacking a methodology, a good man cannot successfully play Iago, nor a bad one Hamlet. For in each instance the actor's personality would comment on the character. The dichotomy between what the character must say and how the actor would react, gesturally, would turn the play into a broad farce, with "Iago" shuddering at his lines, and "Hamlet" sneering at them.

All this resolves itself to the broadly based problem, for the actor, of communicating words (an actor's enemy), in themselves fixed and non-

living, in all their "emotional meaning" to an audience. If the actor
is _to be_ a dynamically active character, not just a "type," he must feel
not what is happening on paper, in lines which he has memorized and which
may or may not mean anything to him, but what is happening within himself,
the living interpreter of the writer's creation. If he fails to become
the character, he necessarily fails to convince his audience that the
stage is peopled by living, completely human characters. And he may find
himself trying to play a mad scene, like a paralytic, with half his body
unresponsive, dead, to what he is trying to be.

It isn't, I think, unreasonable to demand that an actor get into and
understand a character before he tries _to be_ the character. And while
the System may help, it nevertheless deals largely with the conscious
actions and superobjectives, overlooking possible conflicting unconscious
actions on the character's part. It taps what it does of the unconscious
primarily through physical actions and sense and emotional exercises.
And these, without an objectifying theory of personality, depend mostly
on the actor's intuition, as Stanislavski said himself.

When I first undertook to offer the actor a more objective standard for
character analysis, I realized that a thorough and completely objective
study would require films of rehearsals, closed circuit television, and
a full dress production of whatever play I worked on. Lacking equipment
and money, I instead tried to be my own subject, to act (with ten or so
student actors who assisted me in the experiment) and to observe myself,
as an actor must, relying on my familiarity with the theories and techniques of self-analysis to see my way clear. Tape recordings were used,
too, to further objectify what occurred.

For the study I followed Stanislavski as the artistic communicator of a dramatic character to which psychoanalytic principles (dream analysis, recurring symptoms, continuity of analysis, projections, repression, and recording of associations) could be applied. I used Karen Horney's theory of personality not because her methodology is the best or the only one available, but because it seemed at the time the most accessible to the actor, and because I saw a relationship between hers and Stanislavski's System in the character moves and obvious physicalization, as well as a clear parallel between her concept of the "idealized image" and Stanislavski's "magic if."[1]

Again for accessibility, I analyzed Willy Loman, from Miller's Death of a Salesman, though I might note here that the procedures I will outline roughly can be applied to any coherently written character in dramatic literature.

In keeping with Stanislavski's sequence in Creating a Role,[2] I first "told the story of the plot" to gain a knowledge of the given circumstances, and to establish the present tense of the play for myself. The first stage of the study also hinted, occasionally, at Willy's past life. Further, I noted the external objects of the play, I would have to carry, for instance, two heavy valises. What was in them? I would have to answer this question and many others to be a believable character.

Here, in Step One, both Stanislavski and Horney stress the need for a historical approach to the character, and feel that a student must adequately understand the cultural factors which channel behavior into recognizable patterns. Stanislavski, however, does not cover conflict-and-anxiety factors in character evolution. And even in the first step, Horney probes more deeply, and offers greater insights into, key areas like love, sexuality, and **aggression**, so that the actor who understands psychoanalysis has from the start a heightened awareness of the cultural factors which guide neurotic or normal development, and can set his factual material into a frame for the character.

Utilizing, then, what I knew of the play's present tense, of dress, attitudes, etc., I began to discover the character's subtext, the feelings his words connoted, his motives, manner of walking--I read between the lines.

From here, I proceeded to "play the external plot in terms of physical action." In Step Two, Stanislavski hoped to bridge the separation between external and internal. "Enter a room," he writes. "But since you cannot enter unless you know where you came from, where you are going, and why, seek out the external facts of the plot to give you a basis for physical action."[3]

After studying the part for a week, I held a rehearsal with the cast and worked over the physical actions outlined in the play. Wherever the script omitted data or, at the least, allowed me to create actions suitable to the role, I tried to create them. Not surprisingly, though, I found that my performance was at best superficial. Only where the script clearly directed me to open, shut, or handle something, did I find it possible to act believably. In fact, I felt most comfortable and closest to the truth when I carried in the heavy valises, if only because their weight tired me, and made me _feel_ like the sixty year-old man Willy is.

100

It was in the second step that the two systems began to diverge; more clearly, Stanislavski assumed that the physicalization of events would in itself begin to give an actor the essential _feel_ of what is happening. And wrongly so. For learning need not depend on doing a specific something; high-motivation, like grief or excitement, may result in minimal activity, or even in paralysis, while heightened activity may indicate a lowering of tension, of what we call "motivation."[4]

I began, then, to find Horney's theories especially significant to my understanding of Willy's character, the more so because so many of Willy's actions seemed disoriented (or not goal-oriented) or distorted by the freer time and spatial constructs of the dream state.

I noticed first Willy's constant shifting of direction; because I could delineate moves toward objects and, at the same time, sense the reason for Loman's moves against these objects, I could start getting to the center of his conflict. The first scene, for instance, can look like a two-action, two-objective scene. (Willy wants to get some rest and to solve the Big problem.) But when I looked more closely at his moves toward and against various objects and people, I realized that there was an unconscious, or non-conscious element which was operating with, and influencing, his conscious behavior, and that his were not two separate coexisting objectives; they emanated from one basic conflict.

I might mention here that because both methodologies are process systems, It was impossible to prevent elements of later steps from cropping up from the very beginning. While Stanislavski urges the actor, as the second step, to play the plot in terms of physical action only, I soon found myself getting somewhat ahead of his projected scheme of things. For one thing, it is probably asking too much (or too little) for a person to play a scene first intellectually, for gross content, then physically, and finally, for its emotional meaning. Working and experiencing on many levels, a sensitive person, aided by the insights supplied by psychoanalysis, is bound at least intellectually to jump ahead of the System in his understanding of motivation, though, as I pointed out, I felt that I was lagging emotionally because, even with the aid of psycho-analysis, I felt I did not yet know Willy well enough.

In the third step, Stanislavski urges the actor to improvise situations dealing with the character's past and with his anticipated future. It is most importantly the actor's task to create a living, believable past and a possible, imagined future.

In investigating Willy's past, I again found Horney most helpful. For without a technique to treat the dreams in the play with, I, or any actor, would have been unable to make a coherent frame for the character form. By analytically dealing with compression, substitution, and other dream elements, I was able to create a believable pattern which could be acted organically. And it is worth mentioning here that because Stanislavski cannot conceive of a non-productive aspect of the imagination, the actor oriented only to the System must have difficulty in handling later steps of the character's evolution. The simple, linear, conscious System must eventually become as much a hindrance as a help to the actor.

In my work sheets on the dreams, I realized that the injurious effect of Loman's fantasies is that, for one thing, he is not aware that he's daydreaming. As I studied the dreams more closely, I began to get deeper

into Willy's motives.

> Work Sheet #3, first dream (from a tape-recording)
>   I congratulate Biff and Happy about the simoni-
> zing job they've done on the car...Simultaneous with
> my congratulations is my desire to obtain respect and
> love from the boys. I am displaying my know-how to
> them...

And so on. I separated this scene into fourteen parts, using the first

person in my work sheets to avoid, in what I hoped would be a process

of organic character development, a shifting point of reference, and to

suspend the artificial duality of subject-object separation. Here, once

again, an actor unacquainted with psychoanalysis is constantly deflected

by Loman's "idealized image" of "Willy the Salesman" from getting at the

core of Willy the man's personality.

In Step Four, "telling the story of the plot in greater detail," I did

further imaginary exercises, recalling what Biff had looked like when I

had bought the house, in 1921, and what he and the neighborhood had looked

like in 1929, the time of the dream sequences: there were fewer apart-

ment houses, then, and I didn't feel hemmed in by the bricks and windows

I mention in Scene I.

By the third rehearsal, I had filled in many of the given circumstances

of the play, and had practiced sense and emotional exercises. I had

further, in my work sheets, analyzed many of Willy's (my) associations,

so that I was able to begin constructing my superobjective.

I realized, for instance, that flowers and seed planting were symbolic of growth, for me. I desired to make something, particularly my sons grow. And I remembered that Ben had given me a "bunch of wild flowers" before he went to Alaska and to his later success.

I remembered, too, that Ben had told me that father "would start in Boston, and he'd toss the whole family into the wagon, and then he'd drive the team right across the country...And we'd stop in the towns and sell the flutes that he'd made on the way." (The flute music. Do I hear it, or is it just that I want to hear it?) Now, more than before, I understood why I wanted to be a "salesman," the romance the term held for me. And I began to feel the deep contempt for myself that I felt when my relationship with Biff, my future, had been undermined in Boston.

Further, I began to understand my complete dejection at the end of the second dream sequence in Act I. I had failed to measure up to my diamond image--to Ben's success, to one sense--and when Linda jarred me out of my dream, I struck out at the stifling yard and the apartment houses (Willy: Gotta break your neck to see a star in this yard.) I realized suddenly that Biff was my star, the star I couldn't reach, the projection of my failure as the idealized salesman. (Willy: God Almighty, he'll (Biff) be great yet. A star like that, magnificent, can never really fade away!)

I found, in this part of my study, however, that Stanislavski's use of sense and emotional memory, because it neglected central factors in behavior, was of little use, in itself, to me. Without a certain knowledge of the compliant, aggressive, and detached personality, the actor regardless of his memories, cannot play true to the part. Had I, for

for instance, tried to neatly fuse all the discordant aspects of Willy's personality, I would have been prevented, even with the help of sense and emotional memories, from tapping the spontaneous impulses in both myself and the script.

Advancing to Step Five, I now began to form a clearer conception of the superobjective. It was here that the System was most clearly lacking. Michael Chekov's analysis of Willy reveals the System's limitations strikingly.

> What, for instance, would Willy the Salesman look like
> and what would he do were he to become notorious over
> his destiny? His ideal would perhaps resemble the life
> of Dave Singleman in the same play...and if in addition
> to this ideal Willy could have a radio, and a small
> kitchen garden, and be "well-liked" he would feel
> entirely happy. So the super-objectives for him may be
> defined as: "I want to live like that old Dave Singleman."[5]

Dave, it is worth noting, has no fixed residence, and consequently no kitchen garden.

At all events, Chekhov's analysis is just _too_ simple. This single objective, to "live like that old Dave Singleman," would hardly permit the actor to portray Willy in the diversity of his character. Stanislavski posits one superobjective for the character in a drama, but he neglects the unconscious. A good actor must understand that a part of the unconscious (repression) can be brought up to consciousness and that, if he is to play a character realistically, he must attempt to incorporate his unconscious goal (so far as possible) into his part, utlizing all the techniques at his disposal. And having incorporated the character's drives into the automatic layer of his personality, the actor can then

devote himself fully to the conscious superobjective and action. Sense
and emotional memory are then infinitely more relevant to the character's
evolution than they would be to the actor who attempts to play the character as if neither he nor the character had an unconscious. Intuition
alone will not solve the problems involved in an intricate character
analysis.

In the sixth step in Creating a Role, the formation of the superobjective,
I had only to analyze Willy's (my) language, noting the general agitation,
the violence, of my expressions ("to make a hit," "knock 'em dead," etc.)
In killing myself, I knock down the barriers to my "success." If, then,
my conscious objective was to be loved, to be well-liked, my unconscious
objective was to be "big," to be powerful. In finally analyzing myself,
I realized that my desires to be loved and to be "big" had merged into a
need for a sort of reverence. In fact, one reason I could not get along
with Biff was that I could not accept the fact that he could love me, and
yet not idolize me. A second reason was, as I've said, that I had projected my hopes for success onto him, and he had failed. Here, then, was
my tragedy: I had rejected my real self, my actual ability to get along
with the boys, to work with my hands, and had become alienated from the
boys, from Linda and from myself.

The tragedy of Willy Loman is that at the core of his personality he is
unrelated to others and to himself. Because his personality has elements
of expansiveness and self-effacement, he veers between a glorified picture and a detested image of himself. His total identification with one
or the other self entails not only conflicting self-evaluations, but
conflicting behaviors, values, drives, and kinds of satisfactions. When,

as in the dreams, these two ways of experiencing himself occur simultaneously, Loman begins to quiver with tension. And because _he_, Willy the man, never emerges from the dream with an acceptance of the contradictions there as his own, because he cannot really tell the difference between dreaming and not dreaming, the conflicts which eventually drive him to suicide have eaten away his real potentialities long before that final act.[6]

In analyzing Willy Loman, I have tried to emphasize that my reliance on Horney's system is not the final answer. Her methodology seems right now the best one available for the actor, though it will doubtless soon be superseded, what with the rapid advances in medicine and analysis today. What I think is important is that implied in the convergence between psychoanalysis and acting is the recognition that all fields are converging, and that the actor may someday rely on the biochemist's work on DNA for a suitable analysis of character traits.

We must realize that, as McLuhan has said, "those who are concerned with the program 'content' of the media and not with the medium proper appear to be in the position of physicians who ignore the 'syndrome of just being sick.'"[7] We must, as Donald Freed writes, ask the question of the depth psychologists, 'What's going on here?'"[8] And we must not let the arbitrary labels "art" and "science" hinder our answering that question.

1. See, eg., Karen Horney, <u>Neurosis and Human Growth</u> (New York: W. W. Norton and Co., 1950).

2. Constantin S. Stanislavski, <u>Creating a Role</u> (New York: Theatre Arts Books, 1961), p. 252.

3. <u>Ibid</u>.

4. For more discussion on this point, see O. Hobart Mowrer, <u>Learning Theory and Behavior</u> (London: John Wiley and Sons, Inc., 1960), p. 227.

5. Michael Chekov, <u>To the Actor</u> (New York: Harper and Brothers, 1953), p. 158f.

6. Loman's thesis, "I was right! I was right!" indicates two things. First, the tense is the past form "was," and second, these words appear not only in the dream, but outside it. This would indicate that the actual conclusion of the dream and the beginning of Willy's reawareness of the present have not been differentiated from one another.

7. Marshall McLuhan, <u>Understanding Media: The Extensions of Man</u> (New York: McGraw-Hill, 1965), p. 64.

8. Donald Freed, <u>Freud and Stanislavski</u> (New York: Vantage Press, 1964), p. 22. Freed's work is, perhaps, a bit too oriented toward the infantile sexual response of the character (as contrasted to the "historic approach") to be of practical use.

DRAMA THERAPY FOR YOUNG PEOPLE

by Kurt Cerf

In the fall of 1968 I had an interview with William Main, then director
of the Children's Treatment Center at Central State Hospital in Louisville, Kentucky.[1] We discussed the possibility of my conducting drama
classes for the young adult patients at the Center. Mr. Main was
acquainted with my work as director of the Louisville Children's Theatre
and the regular drama workshops I had been conducting for children and
teenagers. Through the generosity of the Younger Woman's Club of St.
Matthews, Mr. Main was able to set up a six-week trial program. If the
results warranted it, the state's Department of Mental Health agreed to
consider to continue the program after the trial period. Classes were
set up for two mornings a week. One of the most important features of
the program was the eager willingness of three of the young people's
instructors in other subjects, to accept my invitation to participate

[1]
    The author wishes to express his gratitude for the helpful guidance he
    received from Dr. Gary May, Kentucky Deputy Commissioner of Psychiatric
    Services for Children.

as students in the drama classes. This had a number of beneficial effects. It permitted me to utilize a variety of "team combinations" in the game-exercises I introduced. A patient, encountering temporary difficulties in working with his peers, could be induced to get on the floor with an instructor he got along with. Sometimes, two instructors would get an exercise going that patients showed reluctance to try. Also, the instructors were helpful in handling outbreaks of aggressive behavior that occurred occasionally during the first few weeks of the course. They were interested to learn the application of drama techniques in the teaching of their own subjects and were able to give running reports on the young patients at meetings of the members of the entire therapy team.

At the time we started the drama course, the treatment center was being renovated. The only room available was small, damp and cluttered with all kinds of objects that proved most distracting. In other subjects, the patients' classes were kept down in number. The young people found it very difficult to relate to and get along with one another even in small groups. Since drama was the one class in which all the twelve young people were together, the classroom atmosphere was negative. In the beginning of the course it alternated between "icy wind" and "volcanic outbreak." There were a few bad fights and the instructors, worrying about my welfare, suggested that I might try lion taming as a safer activity. But even though the patients were letting me and one another know in no uncertain (scatological) terms that they were not going to cooperate in "doing this stuff," I knew from past experience that drama therapy can succeed if one can put to work the key pedagogical ingredients: Love and respect for young people and dramatic imagination.

After a month the patients began to listen and to try some of the game-exercises in earnest. The six trial weeks were nearly over when we had our first real breakthrough. During a portion of each lesson, we had been attempting to rehearse a sketch. The story of the little scene dealt with a young man who had been turnd into a scarecrow by a magic spell and could become human again only if a girl could love him and tell him that she did. I shall not forget Ralph's[2] pitiful, pinched face as he stood crucified against the wall, a perfect scarecrow nailed to the farmer's fence. I knew that Fanny had had a bad fight with Ralph earlier that morning, but she was the only one showing any inclination to play the part of the girl. During previous rehearsals, the students had interrupted with derisive remarks and "wrong" laughs. They had seemed to leave my suggestions unheeded. I was about to switch to other work when I saw something in Fanny's face that I had not seen there before: A faint smile. I went over to her, held her face in my hands for a few moments and said: "I think you might enjoy playing this scene today. Try." Fanny went up to Ralph and looked at him. A new kind of silence arose in the room. Though her back was turned to us, we sensed that she was doing a good job of acting. She was making spontaneous discoveries in character. Ralph really "listened" to her. Usually, he would avert his eyes when talking to people and he did so now while playing the scene with Fanny but this didn't seem to matter as a scarecrow. At the end, Fanny made an awkward little curtsey that had a strange kind of buoyant flair. Then she went close to Ralph, put her cheek next to his in what appeared to be a simulated kiss and whispered, "I love you." Ralph sprang off the wall as if shot from a cannon, and ran around the room shouting, "I'm

---

[2] The real names of patients described in this article have not been used.

free--I'm free" amidst much applause and wholesome laughter. When I con-
gratulated him on his performance, he smiled while crying and I realized
for the first time that he had blue eyes. Soon after this, we were able
to move the class to a bright room with daylight and our work improved
considerably. After the trial period was over, the Department of Mental
Health of the state did continue the program with the utilization of a
federal education grant.

Drama experiences can enhance personality development in the disturbed
young person. Both role playing as well as functional technique exercises can be valuable aids in realization of self and in making contact
with others. I use the same exercises in working with mental patients
that I employ in the training of actors. However, for rate of progress,
I put no pressure whatsoever on disturbed students. Participation is
always voluntary. For good training in social skills, the students
should not only be motivated but should be "group motivated." I try to
induce this in a number of ways. The students always sit in a semi-
circle of chairs in front of the stage (or stage area). At all times
they are encouraged to be in touch with one another as well as with the
actors onstage. If possible, I try to turn negative behavior into posi-
tive learning. For example, the second year of our drama program we
were fortunate to be able to use the stage of the multi-purpose auditorium
at Central State Hospital. Having a piano, stage lights and a curtain
available, made up for the occasional distractions caused by the athletic equipment in the large hall. At the beginning of one of the early
sessions in the "gym-theatre," the young people were "horsing around"
with various equipment. They were supposed to bring their chairs from
the storage area and set them down in front of the stage in the above-

mentioned semi-circle. I called the class into session three times. No cooperation was forthcoming. I checked my watch and "just sat." The "athletes" had expected me to get increasingly more impatient with them but I didn't and they eventually joined the drama class. When the last one had brought his chair over and had sat down, I checked my watch again and before we started our work I announced quietly that twelve minutes had been wasted and that I thought we had agreed that the gym equipment would be used only during the gym periods. Toward the end of that particular drama session, the entire group happened to be doing an improvisation that worked extremeley well. Everyone wanted to "do it again." But I looked at my watch and informed the students that the session was over. "Why - why - there is still time," they exclaimed. "Yes, I said. Ten minutes. I choose to take back the time you owe me right now. Good morning." I left, pondering the horrid names they were calling me behind my back. However, thereafter, the gym equipment seemed to have lost its attraction during drama class.

Motivation cannot be commanded. It ought to be induced. It needs to be permitted to grow on its own momentum and should be nurtured with loving care like the tending of a growing plant. Phil's experience may serve as an example here. He joined the drama class at the time we were beginning to use the auditorium. After entering, he would walk about the large space, head bowed, in an obsessive compulsive manner and would finally sit down in a far-away corner. Sometime during each session we would take a ten-minute break during which I would go over and would try to make contact with Phil. Between September and May, Phil went through the following stages:

113

No response; Shaking head when invited to sit nearer to stage area; Nodding head when told that he could come nearer whenever he would be ready; Responding to greeting with nod of head but still not speaking; Bringing his chair fifty feet closer to stage but going back to corner after intermission ended; Beginning to sit closer; Responding to greeting with whispered "Hello," head still bowed; Responding to greeting and and making eye contact; Sitting about ten feet behind circle of chairs with head bowed; Engaging in brief conversation while permitting my arm around his shoulder; Sitting at outside of semi-circle and watching work occasionally; Talking freely with me but refusing to participate in work. During the break of the very last session that spring, I asked Phil if he would do the class a favor. He said he would try. I didn't tell him then what the favor was but when the session resumed after the break, I announced it: "Phil is going to do the 'Statue-Reflex' exercise for us." I knew from his past reactions that Phil enjoyed watching the others do this exercise. To do it well required good concentration and practice. Phil went up on the stage and did the exercise - well. So far as I could find out, this was the first time he had ever tried it. It seems that all along some sort of "perceptual osmosis" must have been at work. While Phil had wanted to do the exercise for some time, he was able to participate actively only when he felt that he was ready to do so. He then got real enjoyment out of his achievement.

Motivation can be induced also by leading the students to awareness of the needs of others. Making a student laugh at his own shortcomings can be helpful here. While working with one or more students onstage, I often turn to whomever may be causing a disturbance in the auditorium with

114

a remark like this: "You two, if you're trying to disrupt our work, you'll have to talk much louder. We can't make out what you're whispering." This usually amuses everybody and restores attention. Unless the students are fully motivated, they gain little if anything from drama exercises. In teaching disturbed young people, directions and suggestions must be adjusted to the individual, moment by moment, even within the same session. The experience should be fun. "Hard work fun," not "horsing around." The training should lead the students to make spontaneous discoveries, not encourage them to perform to impress others. Too many acting teachers lead their students to surface and mechanical effects by asking them to "show us." This method is counter to encouraging creative function and total involvement.

Mr. Marc Cummings, the young teacher who has worked with the class from the beginning of the drama program at Central State Hospital, has kindly given me permission to quote him here: "During rather dull weekends and evenings, the young people frequently involved themselves in drama games. That is, when staff were not for some reason involved with the kids, they themselves turned to drama. And they could turn to drama because they possessed the intuitive understanding that drama would work, the understanding if the improvisation or skit was not successful from a technical or theatrical standpoint, it was, nevertheless, fun. Fun, at a state institution for disturbed children is often not present. Mr. Cerf's approach does not include fear or any kind of authoritarianism. Drama is the only area of our program where all the young people learn to work together without fear. In class the students show little of the teasing and embarrassment associated with adolescence. The spirit of learning and the non-fearful technique allows them to accept the poor

115

actors in the class. Teasing because of lack of drama ability is prac-
tically non-existent."

The drama experience should realize these objectives: Unstrained use
of the voice, total relaxation, free expression of creative imagination,
heightened sensory perception, ability to concentrate, ease in rhythmic
explorations, courage to try something new, sense of being appreciated
by peers and teacher, appreciation of the skills of others and the
ability to criticize constructively. Exercises should build gradually
into improvisations and scene work. Here a few samples will have to
suffice. For full oxygen intake and as preamble to total relaxation, I
encourage breathing with the diaphragm. We do the "Balloon Game." My
arm becomes a giant's pump handle. We take the air in through the nose
and make it flow out smoothly through the open mouth. Then we count
from one to ten, using a full breath for each number, starting with
voiceless whisper and ending with top voice energy but without screaming
or straining. We make sure that we permit each student his or her particular level of capability. Recently, a student ventured beyond the
exercise by shouting "eleven" after all others had stopped as usual at
"ten." It is remarkable to note that this patient was unable to participate in _any_ exercise a year ago as she was almost completely out of
touch with reality. After we have accomplished reasonably good voice
relaxation, we practice changing voice energy levels at will. I call
out the level (between one and ten) as the students now count continuously. Then we add a concentration training feature. We count continuously and on different voice levels while I try to distract the students.
Now they stand in a semi-circle with individuals counting as I point
at them. The moment I point at someone else, the firt "counter" must

stop, even in the middle of the word, and the student now pointed at
must finish that word and continue counting, and on various voice levels
as called for by me. The next time we might be ready to add the ingre-
dient of imagination to the exercise. Instead of counting, we now tell
a simple story. This "Chain Story" can be an actual occurrence, fantasy
or a combination of both. All it needs is some kind of continuity when
picked up by the next student pointed to. Difficulty in continuing the
story of someone else is encountered when the students are unable to
listen "organically." To bring this home, we often do basic pantomime
exercises here. We handle ice cubes to realize their "full dramatic
image." We look at a picture of a snake and handle a rope which reminds
us of a snake's body until we can recreate a snake in pantomime through
sense memory. In the "Chain Story" exercise it is necessary that the
instructor recognize from the facial expressions of the students whether
or not they are listening with their whole being and trying to re-live
the story that is told by someone else. When they can do this, picking
up someone else's story is merely the verbal continuation of their own
inner experience.

It must be remembered that all drama exercise-games should be processes
rather than performance results. For the student who is learning to
play the piano, scales are not music. Playing them is done to improve
digital dexterity and, in time, to permit the pianist to draw the sense
of the piano into his kinesthesia. The same is true in acting training.
If the student is encouraged to work from the skin inwards, chances are
good that he will find who he "inly is." The "Chain Story" exercise can
be developed into scene work by the students' choosing a particularly
good invention and working it up through improvisation into a written

and rehearsed scene.

We approach total relaxation by exercises combining reflex practice with deep breathing. I use a drum for this work. It encourages rhythmic expression and can be employed to help varying the heartbeat. The students sort themselves out on the studio floor. I like to tell them to find the spot that has their name written on it. When the drum sounds, they imagine that a friendly hand grenade has exploded within them without causing any harm, or that they are soft clay and a giant sculptor has picked up their lump and suddenly formed a statue. This statue must not move until the drum suddenly sounds again, and again they explode into an unanticipated form. The students don't mind when I walk about among them and give them a sudden shove as I hit the drum. We look for a whip-like reaction here, not a fancy ballet movement, thought out in advance. Having achieved a reasonably good amount of freedom of movement from the base of the spine, we lie on the floor, on our backs. We do some deep breathing and add a free vocalized sigh to the exhalation. Sighing is a natural way to release tension and it induces relaxation, especially with deep breathing. After a few minutes of this, I ask the students to breath normally, that is, without special attention to their breathing and we do some exercises that accelerate blood circulation. In one of these, I ask them to imagine that the same giant who previously sculptured them, is now suddenly throwing them into a deep-freezer at fifty degrees below zero when I hit the drum. Naturally, the body contracts and every muscle is tensed. I walk about the classroom to check if I can move any arms, heads or legs. If I can, I might have to "cut them off." As soon as body vibration sets in, we let go completely. We wiggle every part, not vigorously but very, very gently. We try to think of different parts of the body as untying themselves from within. Now we might be ready to combine the Balloon game with the total tension and soft relaxation exercise. Again, we make sure not to strain. We let the air go out with a vocalized sigh and wiggle gently the very moment we release from tension. We not try for total relaxation. We add imagination. The students lie flat on the floor, doing absolutely nothing but breathing normally. They execute nothing physically, but are asked to listen to and to imagine the story I am telling them. At the beginning of the story I beat the drum fairly quickly and then, gradually, I slow the beats down. To avoid hypnotic trance, I weave "awareness factors" into the story the students are to imagine. Though the content of the story comes from me, the students' involvement is self-directed. I tell them: "You are dreaming you are lying on a pleasant beach on a sunny day, enjoying the feeling of the warm sand beneath you. Soon, you are completely relaxed, breathing normally, without a care in the world. Now you are beginning to notice a strange sensation: Your body seems to feel very heavy. It is getting heavier and heavier until all your bones seem to be dissolved and your body feels like a warm puddle of soft material, making a mold in the sand. The base of your spine is now unlocked, unlocked, unlocked. With your head remaining outside on a pillow of sand, the rest of your body seems to sink now into the sand very, very slowly and it is getting heavier and heavier." All during this, the drum beats have slowed down. Now, they phase out completely and we have a minute of silence. Varying with the circumstances, Imight now lead the students through an internal improvisation which encourages them to feel themselves as light balloons and stop the improvisation with that sensation or ask them quietly to sit up and try to retain the heavy state as long as possible.

Some students may have gone to sleep and require much time to collect themselves. No one should be rushed. A quiet discussion period in which those who wish to talk are encouraged to do so, is usually the best way to end a lesson. The material that will be verbalized is often remarkably revealing, especially in the case of mental patients. At Central State Hospital this exercise provides the only time when all the young people are together and completely quiet.

After we have developed sufficient freedom in the basic reflex work, we go to the "Mirror Game." Here, two students face one another, one being the master, the other his mirror. Again using the drum, the master explodes on the beat and the mirror must react at once or consider himself broken. Concentration, motivation and focusing power are the ingredients that can be practiced in this fun game. The master's intent is to break the mirror and the mirror's is to stay alive. After a few statues have been tried and the students have learned to trust their reflexes and have stopped "thinking movement" and have learned just to let go, I call "change," and the mirror moves to the other side. The former mirror now initiates and has a nice chance to get even with his former tormentor. After some practice, the change can go back and forth rapidly, yet the onlooking students will not be able to tell who initiates and who follows. Discussing with the students the miraculous facility of the human body and mind in translating an image into action instantaneously, is a good way to bolster egos and encourage self-confidence. After trying visual reflex, we do the same with oral challenges. Here we use words and numbers, the object being to shoot them past the ear of the oral mirror, who in turn, makes up his mind to bounce the words back before the master has barely pronounced them. This exercise is great fun and an

120

excellent tool in helping students to relate to one another totally.
Soon we are ready for all kinds of combinations. One student can be
the visual master while his partner follows him, providing oral challenges at the same time. From single words one can go to story telling
and even singing the story to be reproduced by the mirror. These exercises reveal all types of blocked areas in mental patients and progress
is often slow. Intermediate steps and auxiliary processes will have to
be invented by the teacher to fill in and bring along students who have
difficulties. Again quoting Mr. Cummings, he says "I have found this
to be an especially pleasing way to relate to the young people because
often their good coordination and perceptual ability means that they
out-perform me. I prefer this kind of friendly competition to the
typical competition between student and teacher."

After the Mirror Game, creative imagination and free interplay should be
added to reflex practice. This is the exercise Phil did for the class.
Here, the student goes thorugh a number of reflex statues until I stop
him when an interesting one turns up for him to justify. He now holds
this statue. We imagine that a movie camera has stopped suddenly and
has caught him in this position. He must now fill in a story that has
happened and has made this position necessary. Everyone is challenged
to invent a fitting story but the initiator of the statue chooses the
idea he wishes to act out. When he is ready, someone call "Warning"
and "Curtain" and now the statue comes to life and continues the scene.
Here we phase in what we call a "Time, Place and Space Investigation."
The student tries to create honestly the atmosphere of the imagined place,
tries to "personalize" characters he needs to invent because they belong
in his scene and tries to find a strong motivation with which to function

naturally in the forthcoming improvisation. If, for instance, he is
bringing to life a statue that is lying on the floor with hands reaching
upward, he might decide that he had just been knocked down. In the pre-
curtain preparation he must create fully the person who knocked him
down. The idea of a general adversary will not do. He must "substitute
images," find someone or a combination of persons wrapped into one who
will fit his opponent. The more sensory his association, the truer will
be the identification. I recall one instance wherein the student told
the class after the exercise that "The guy who knocked me down smelled
of cigar ashes." This remark was interesting and I reported it to the
boy's doctor who knew immediately that the character in question was the
boy's father who had been "knocking him down" in every sense of the word
before the young man had been hospitalized. In the psychodrama approach
the teacher might have probed for the father substitution then and there.
But this might have done more harm than good. There are so many shadings
and subtle vibrations of behavior a mental patient seems to need to cover
up his embarrassing condition, that shock therapy does not have a
lasting therapeutic answer for. I have seen a psychodrama session in
which the person in charge shook a patient violently by the shoulders,
all the while shouting, "I'm your father and I hate you, I hate you."
Truly, this created shock for the patient. He was hurt and embarrassed.
Even if the operator were a superb actor and could create the semblance
of the cruel father's image, such re-enactment in front of others could
never be completely believable to the patient. He feels (or should feel)
that the operator cares for him. Being shocked into thinking that he is
confronted by his father was cruel. This knowledge is no passport to
resolving his deeply hidden emotional problems. On the other hand, in
role playing, the patient often resolves an emotional problem while he

122

is comfortably hiding behind his face-saving shield, without even knowing that he is working on his therapy. Properly reported out, further revelations can be made with the help of the therapist as he probes the material in his private session with the patient. This game-exercise (Bringing a Statue to Life) can be carried into group improvisation when the students are ready for this. Here a scene that has been started by one student is "peopled" by the characters he needs in it by the other students. They raise their hands as they have "personalized" the character they think the initiator needs and I send them into the scene. Often, the entire class gets drawn into a group improvisation which may take up the major portion of that session. Sometimes the students write up a scene together at a social session that had originated as an exercise in class. The group at Central State Hospital has been eager to perform a very funny scene called "Hitler's Big Move," for three years, even though the original initiator has long been dismissed from the hospital and only two patients of the first group are still in the class. Creative explorations that are repeated voluntarily by the students outside of class are not only therapeutic but also enriching.

We often do a game called "Two Drunks on a Park Bench." Two actors sit on a bench and relax completely. When the curtain goes up they may be "asleep" or in a "drunken stupor." They then play out any fantasy situation which they invent on the spot. There is only one rule: They must deal with one another's inventions and relate to the situations fully; either accepting or rejecting them. This exercise brings to the surface many personality problems. For example, Fanny had left the park bench and was groping along a wall; eyes closed, when she came upon a shelf and picked up a small object. She opened her eyes to find a small doll in her hand. At once she said to the doll: "Oh mother, what are you doing here?" She then tossed the doll into a corner violently. Subsequently, her therapist made use of this incident in her session with Fanny. The park bench exercise can also be utilized as a group improvisation, starting with two or more drunks and having additional characters join the scene as it unfolds.

When the patients are ready for it, I encourage them to try out for parts in the Louisville Children's Theatre's regular productions in town. I find that the experience of being turned down can be as beneficial in one way as the one of being accepted and cast can be in another. Betty had been going to high school away from the hospital for a month when tryouts came up for one of our plays. She had been reluctant to continue going to school outside as she claimed that her fellow students ostracised her. It seems that she had been advised at the school to keep her home address a secret. Since this was impossible, she may have created unnecessary problems for herself. She was on the verge of trying to quit school when she came down for the tryouts. We had over a hundred young people trying out that afternoon. Lack of time makes it necessary that we do the first screening in groups. One of the means we employ to get a feeling about the applicants is to ask them to stand on the stage and tell us their name, address, favorite food and hobby. We ask them to express themselves with as much animation as possible. When her turn came, Betty asked me if she could omit her home information. I said "no" and explained to her that anyone in our theatre company who would object to her because she was living in a mental hospital, would not fit into our ensemble as we frown upon prejudice of any kind. It took courage for Betty to go up on that stage in front of all those persons of whom she knew only one, and tell where she lived. Nobody seemed to notice. In fact, some of our really bright young people made friends with Betty shortly after she was cast and invited her to their home. Being absorbed, even only temporarily, in an atmosphere where family love reigned, seemed to have a very beneficial effect on Betty. She found herself sought after socially. Betty did a good job in playing an important role. Since that time there has been no part that was right for her. She asked to work on the stage crew and did very well in that capacity also. Betty has been dismissed from the hospital. While the main credit for her recovery must be given to the excellent care she has received at the treatment center, there can be no doubt that her drama experiences have helped to serve as a bridge to the outside world.

For young people in general, theatre exploration can be a powerful recreational and educational tool on both sides of the curtain. As treatment centers move further and further away from the custodial approach, carefully planned drama activity can be employed as an aid in therapy. It is hoped that the experience is also a factor in the young person's ability to adjust after he or she has left the hospital.